T0244417

Table of Contents

· · ·

WHY WE VOTE

OTHER BOOKS IN THE SERIES:

INALIENABLE RIGHTS SERIES

...

SERIES EDITOR
Geoffrey R. Stone

David A. Strauss
GERALD RATNER DISTINGUISHED SERVICE
PROFESSOR OF LAW
UNIVERSITY OF CHICAGO LAW SCHOOL

Mark V. Tushnet
WILLIAM NELSON CROMWELL
PROFESSOR OF LAW
HARVARD LAW SCHOOL

Kathleen M. Sullivan
STANLEY MORRISON PROFESSOR OF LAW
STANFORD LAW SCHOOL

J. Harvie Wilkinson III
JUDGE
U.S. COURT OF APPEALS FOR THE FOURTH
CIRCUIT

Cass R. Sunstein
ROBERT WALMSLEY UNIVERSITY PROFESSOR
HARVARD LAW SCHOOL

Kenji Yoshino
CHIEF JUSTICE EARL WARREN PROFESSOR OF
CONSTITUTIONAL LAW
NEW YORK UNIVERSITY SCHOOL OF LAW

Laurence H. Tribe
CARL M. LOEB UNIVERSITY
PROFESSOR OF LAW
HARVARD LAW SCHOOL

GEOFFREY STONE AND OXFORD UNIVERSITY PRESS GRATEFULLY ACKNOWLEDGE THE INTEREST AND SUPPORT OF THE FOLLOWING ORGANIZATIONS IN THE INALIENABLE RIGHTS SERIES: THE ALA; THE CHICAGO HUMANITIES FESTIVAL; THE AMERICAN BAR ASSOCIATION; THE NATIONAL CONSTITUTION CENTER; THE NATIONAL ARCHIVES

Why We Vote

Owen Fiss

OXFORD
UNIVERSITY PRESS

OXFORD
UNIVERSITY PRESS

Oxford University Press is a department of the University of Oxford. It furthers
the University's objective of excellence in research, scholarship, and education
by publishing worldwide. Oxford is a registered trade mark of Oxford University
Press in the UK and certain other countries.

Published in the United States of America by Oxford University Press
198 Madison Avenue, New York, NY 10016, United States of America.

© Owen Fiss 2024

Library of Congress Cataloging-in-Publication Data
Names: Fiss, Owen, author.
Title: Why we vote / Owen Fiss.
Description: New York : Oxford University Press, 2024. |
Series: Inalienable rights |
Includes bibliographical references and index. |
Identifiers: LCCN 2023038949 (print) | LCCN 2023038950 (ebook) |
ISBN 9780197746387 (hardback) | ISBN 9780197746400 (epub) |
ISBN 9780197746417
Subjects: LCSH: Suffrage—United States.
Classification: LCC KF4891 .F57 2024 (print) | LCC KF4891 (ebook) |
DDC 342.73/072--dc23/eng/20231002
LC record available at https://lccn.loc.gov/2023038949
LC ebook record available at https://lccn.loc.gov/2023038950

DOI: 10.1093/oso/9780197746387.001.0001

Printed by Sheridan Books, Inc., United States of America

To Bradley Hayes
For all he has done for me and for the life of the Yale Law School.
With admiration and endless gratitude

Series Editor's Foreword

...

In this timely and important book, especially at this moment in history, Owen Fiss, one of our nation's most respected and accomplished scholars, explores the role of the Supreme Court in protecting the fundamental right to vote. As he notes, "elections only generate the freedom that democracy promises if the voters are allowed to choose those they wish to govern." With that in mind, he maintains that an essential role of the Supreme Court in preserving our commitment to democracy is guarding against majorities enacting laws designed to ensure their power at the expense of minorities.

As Fiss notes, beginning in the 1960s we have long counted on the Supreme Court "to give meaning and expression to the public values embodied in the Constitution." Indeed, "starting in the 1960s, the Supreme Court has referred to the right to vote as precious or fundamental." During the era of the Warren Court, for example, the Court embraced the principle of "one person/one vote," held the poll tax unconstitutional, and upheld the constitutionality of the Voting Rights Act of 1965.

In the years since then, however, particularly in recent years, through the Burger, Rehnquist, and Roberts Courts, the Supreme

Court has increasingly abandoned that responsibility and has embraced an interpretation of the right to vote that "distorts the interpretive endeavor" of the Court and "belittles the overarching democratic purposes of the Constitution."

As we move into the future, Fiss shows us how the Supreme Court over the last half-century has too often failed to meet one of its most fundamental responsibilities and allowed a range of manipulative actions by the majority to undermine the essential rights of the minority.

Geoffrey R. Stone
May 2023

Introduction

...

Democracy as a Source of Freedom

THE AMERICAN CONSTITUTION is a constitution of freedom. It promises a democratic system of government and, to the extent that promise is fulfilled, it endows the American people, as a people, with political freedom.[1]

Like any type of government, a democratic government has the authority to issue rules and edicts that bind citizens. In that respect, a democracy is similar to, say, a monarchy, or an autocracy backed by the force of arms, or even a theocracy. A democracy differs, however, by vesting in the people a power to choose their rulers and to hold them accountable for their actions and, in this way, allows its subjects to enjoy a measure of freedom unknown to others. The people, acting as a collectivity, exercise this freedom through the conduct of periodic elections, in which the franchise is distributed to all who are governed and in which individuals are allowed to vote for the candidate they prefer, with each vote counting as much as another.

Why We Vote. Owen Fiss, Oxford University Press. © Owen Fiss 2024.
DOI: 10.1093/oso/9780197746387.003.0001

In addition to establishing the structure of government and making democracy the cornerstone of that structure, the Constitution also establishes a scheme of enumerated liberties, which are, for the most part, listed in the Bill of Rights. In many instances, these enumerated freedoms arise not from any direct or explicit grant by the Constitution but rather as an implication from a specific restraint on governmental action, for example, the prohibition on unreasonable searches and seizures and the rule prohibiting Congress from abridging the freedom of speech. Political freedom—that is, the capacity of those who are ruled to choose their rulers—is of another character altogether. Let us call it a systemic freedom. It is not explicitly conferred to all who are governed, nor is it implied by a prohibition on the exercise of government power. It arises from the very system of government that the Constitution seeks to establish.

The enumerated freedoms that are conferred or granted by the Constitution are usually thought of as entrusting ordinary citizens with rights, for example the right to speak (arising from the First Amendment) or the right to privacy (arising from the Fourth Amendment) or the right to counsel in criminal cases (arising from the Sixth Amendment). Political freedom also gives rise to a right, namely the right to vote, for voting constitutes the essential means through which those who are ruled participate in the process by which their rulers are chosen. This right is not directly or explicitly granted by the Constitution but rather is assumed or necessarily implied from the democratic character of the government it establishes. The right to vote is immanent in the Constitution.

Thus, when the Fifteenth Amendment extended, in 1870, the franchise to the newly freed slaves, it specifically spoke of "the right to vote" as though it already existed and then declared that this right shall not be denied to anyone on the basis of race or previous condition of servitude. A similar assumption is manifest in the rhetorical structure of the Nineteenth Amendment. It does not grant or create the right to vote, but rather, once again, assumes its existence and then declares that it shall not be denied because of sex.

Although individuals decide for whom they will vote, the Constitution is not indifferent as to whether they vote. The Constitution may be indifferent as to whether one of the enumerated rights, such as the right to privacy, the right to speak, or the right to be represented by counsel, are exercised; for this reason, such rights can be waived. This is not true of the right to vote. It belongs to all those who are governed, and it should be exercised by them in order to preserve the democratic character of the government. Individuals pick or choose who they are voting for but are obliged to vote to affirm the importance of democracy and to nourish the democratic character of the government under which they live. The exercise of the right to vote lends credence to the claim of the victor of an election that he or she represents the sentiment of the people. Voting is a civic duty.

The offenses of the angry mob that invaded the Capitol on January 6, 2021, in an effort to prevent Congress from tallying the votes of the Electoral College and thus certifying the election of Joseph Biden and Kamala Harris as President and Vice President of the United States were manifold. These individuals invaded the legislative chamber. They destroyed government property and threatened violence and, in some instances, inflicted it. They interfered with the discharge of governmental duties and threatened to block the election of those persons who were selected by the American people to be their President and Vice President. In all, the action was a threat to our political freedom.

Unlike the mob that stormed the Capitol on January 6, 2021, those who do not vote or refrain from voting do not threaten violence. Nor do they obstruct the functioning of a governmental institution. Yet through their inaction, they too impair the political freedom of America that arises from the democratic character of its government and thus violate their elemental duty of citizenship. We vote to preserve democracy and thus our own freedom.

CHAPTER I

The Constitutional Character of Our Democracy

DEMOCRACY IS A guiding ideal of the Constitution. It sets the standard for judging the adequacy of the governmental structure under which we live and, at the same time, projects into the future what that structure should be. It represents an ideal that is progressively realized, even if it may never be fully realizable. Democracy is, from the perspective of the Constitution, both a mandate and an aspiration.

ORIGINS

The democratic ideal guided the construction of the Constitution of 1787. The Constitution was presented as embodying the work of "We the People," and it came into force only after it was ratified by popular assemblies in the states. The Philadelphia Convention transmitted the draft of the Constitution to the states of the Confederation for ratification and, in so doing, provided that the draft should be considered by "a Convention of Delegates, chosen by each State by

Why We Vote. Owen Fiss, Oxford University Press. © Owen Fiss 2024.
DOI: 10.1093/oso/9780197746387.003.0002

the People thereof under the recommendation of its Legislature." Although the men who forged the draft of the Constitution in Philadelphia provided that the new nation would come into being when popular assemblies in nine states had approved the draft of the Constitution, as it turned out assemblies in all thirteen of the states approved it.

The Constitution divides the national legislature into two chambers and provides that the members of one of them (the House of Representatives) are to be elected "by the People" of the several states. It also specifies that the number of representatives for each state in the House shall be based on state population and further stipulates that "the Electors in each State should have the Qualifications requisite for the Electors of the most numerous Branch of the State Legislature." In addition, Article IV requires the national government to guarantee to every state "a Republican Form of Government."

Over the last two and a half centuries, the Constitution of 1787 has been amended a number of times, and many of these amendments enlarged its democratic character. The Fourteenth Amendment, adopted at the end of the Civil War, provides that every person born in the United States is a citizen of the United States and as such enjoys the privileges and immunities of the citizens of the United States. Section 2 of that amendment provides for sanctions for disenfranchisement and, in so doing, explicitly refers to the "right to vote"—the very first time that the phrase appears in the Constitution—and thus that provision strongly implies that the right to vote is one of the privileges and immunities of citizens of the United States.

Section 2 of the Fourteenth Amendment provides for a reduction of the state's representation as a sanction for interferences with the right to vote and in so many words extends that protection of the right to vote to the election of state as well as federal officials. Two years later, in 1870, the Fifteenth Amendment was adopted to make clear a specific and crucial ambition of the Fourteenth Amendment. It provides that "[t]he right of citizens of the United States to vote shall not be denied or abridged by the United States or by any state on account of race, color, or previous condition of servitude." The essential precondition of the Fifteenth as well as the Fourteenth Amendment was the Thirteenth Amendment, which, in 1865, declared an end to slavery.

The Nineteenth Amendment was adopted in 1920 after a long and determined struggle that had its roots in the nineteenth century.[1] It constitutes yet a further, indeed monumental, instantiation of the democratic ideal. It gave women the right to vote. The Twenty-Fourth and Twenty-Sixth Amendments also extended the franchise. The Twenty-Fourth, adopted in 1964, prohibits denying in elections for federal officials the right to vote for failure to pay a poll tax or, for that matter, any other tax. The Twenty-Sixth, adopted in 1971 in the middle of the Vietnam War and reflecting the scope of the military draft then in effect, extended the franchise by lowering the voting age in all elections to eighteen.

In counterpoint to the slow but certain expansion of the franchise that was guided by the democratic ideal over the last two and a half centuries, the constitutional rule regarding the representation in the Senate—two senators for each state—has remained fixed and thus stands as a feature of the Constitution that makes it impossible, at least within the terms of the Constitution, for the democratic ideal ever to be fully realized. At first, the members of the Senate were elected by the legislatures of the several states. The Seventeenth Amendment, adopted in 1913, provides for the direct election of senators but that amendment did not alter the rule requiring two senators for each state, regardless of its population. Nor would an amendment altering the number of senators so that it would accord with the population of the various states be possible within the scope of Article V. That article specifically provides "that no State, without its Consent, shall be deprived of its equal suffrage in the Senate."

The rule requiring equal suffrage for each state in the Senate is an affront to democratic principles. It should be viewed as an exception defining the outer limit of the democratic ideal, not as a basis for denying or undermining the democratic aspirations of the Constitution taken as a whole. The equal suffrage rule and the provision making it unamendable were the products of a compromise. They were intended to induce the participants in the assemblies that met in each state to ratify the draft of 1787 and thereby surrender a measure of the autonomy that their state enjoyed under the Articles of Confederation. The participants in these popular assemblies were being asked to submit themselves and the officers of their state to the authority of the new national government that the Constitution sought to bring into being. Yet between the special arrangements for the Senate and the announcement of "We the People" lies a vast domain, which, I maintain, is governed by democracy as a guiding or regulatory ideal.

THE RISK OF THE ELECTORAL COLLEGE

The Senate is the Senate and as such should be viewed as a democratic anomaly. Yet the Electoral College, also established by the Constitution in 1787, extends the representational structure of the Senate—two votes for each state—to the election of the President and Vice President. In the Electoral College, each state is given the number of votes equal to the sum of its representatives in both the House of Representatives and the Senate. As a result, although on Election Day Americans vote for the President and Vice President, that expression of the popular will is filtered through the structure of the Electoral College. As a formal matter, victory goes to the candidates who have the most votes in the Electoral College. This threat to the democratic ideal is tempered by a practice—let us call it a constitutional practice—that has evolved over the last two and a half centuries and now prevails in all fifty states. According to this practice, rooted either in statutory enactments or informal social understanding, the members of the Electoral College are required to cast their vote in accordance with the popular vote in their state.

A risk remains, nevertheless, that because of the way the votes in the Electoral College are allocated, state by state, there may be a discrepancy between the popular vote, when viewed on a national level, and the cumulative vote in the Electoral College. As a result, a candidate who has the most votes in the Electoral College may not have won the popular vote aggregated on a national level. On rare occasions, that risk has materialized, as it did in recent memory in the presidential elections of 2000 and 2016. In those elections, the candidates who had won the Electoral College vote and thus the presidency in fact lost the national popular vote. Accordingly, awarding victory in those elections to the candidates who won the most votes in the Electoral College betrayed the democratic ideal. From the perspective of our constitutional tradition, these elections must be regarded from the democratic perspective as aberrations, as malfunctions of the system, though the nation reluctantly acquiesced to the result dictated by the Electoral College.

The risk of such malfunctions would be greater if the Electors were freed from the state laws and social understanding that tether them to the popular vote in the state they represent and were somehow allowed to exercise independent judgment as to who should become President and Vice President. Yet the Supreme Court, in recognition of the democratic ideal and the constitutional practice to which it has given rise, has consistently refused to grant Electors this independence. Indeed, as recently as June 2020, the Court allowed the state of Washington to punish—by the imposition of a so-called civil fine of one thousand dollars—any Elector who claimed for him or herself this independence.[2]

In this particular case, Justice Elena Kagan, who wrote for the Court, made it abundantly clear that the ruling was predicated not on a deference to the states as a tribute to their sovereignty, but rather on a desire to further the democratic aspiration of the Constitution. She described Electors as nothing more than "agents of others" and characterized the state rule requiring Electors to follow the popular vote in the state as a way of denying Electors the power to reverse "the vote of millions of its citizens."[3] Referring to the common practice requiring the Electors to honor the popular vote in the state, Justice Kagan, speaking on behalf of a remarkably unanimous Court, concluded: "That direction accords with the Constitution—as well as with the trust of a nation in that here, We the People rule."[4] In a related case, the Court upheld the power of Colorado to replace an Elector who threatened to cast a ballot for a candidate who did not win the popular vote.[5]

In the election of 2020, as opposed to the elections of 2000 and 2016, there was no discrepancy, viewed on a national level, between the popular vote and the vote in the Electoral College. Joseph Biden and Kamala Harris won both. In December 2020, soon after the election and the result of that election becoming clear, the losing candidate for the presidency, the incumbent President Donald Trump, demanded that his Vice President, Mike Pence, deliver him a victory through the exercise of his responsibility in the Electoral College. The Vice President is designated by the Constitution to chair the joint session of the House and Senate that is to receive and tabulate the votes of the Electoral College.

At the joint session of Congress, representatives of the various states were to present Vice President Pence slates of Electors that were certified by each state governor to be in accord with the popular vote in that state. Trump's supporters had prepared alternative slates of electors who pledged to support Trump even though he had not won the popular vote in these states and the alternative slates were not certified by the governors of those states. Such alternative slates were prepared for Arizona, Georgia, Michigan, Nevada, New Mexico, Pennsylvania, and Wisconsin. Under this scheme, the alternative slates were to be presented to Pence on the assumption that they would be sufficient basis for Pence to put off certifying the victory of Biden and Harris. Still, it is not at all clear how Pence was to use his powers to turn a defeat of Biden and Harris into a victory for Trump and Pence.

Conceivably, the delay in certifying the election results might have enabled Trump to make a last ditch effort to contest the outcome in the targeted states. Or Trump may have even been banking on the joint session of Congress to accept the alternative slates of Electors even though they had not been certified by the governors, thereby selecting him and Pence as the victors of the 2020 election. The Electoral Count Act of 1887 empowers this joint session of Congress to determine which votes should be counted whenever it concludes that the Electoral College slates representing the winning candidates were not "legally certified" or "regularly given."

Pence balked. Well aware of the fact that Trump's challenge to the popular votes in the states in question was rejected by every court to which it was presented, Pence refused to accede to Trump's demand. Even the Supreme Court denied, for lack of standing, an application by the state of Texas for leave to file a complaint challenging the results in Georgia, Michigan, Pennsylvania, and Wisconsin.[6] Accordingly, Pence viewed his role in purely ministerial terms—not to second-guess the popular vote in the various states or to contest their certification, but simply to receive and tabulate the votes of the electors that were officially certified in each state and then, in the joint session, presented to him.

Rebuffed by Pence, Trump scheduled a rally to be held at the Ellipse, just outside the White House grounds and adjacent to the National Mall. He scheduled it for January 6, 2021, the day Congress was scheduled to certify the votes of the Electoral College and thus approve the election of Biden and Harris. Egged on by Trump at this rally and by some of his followers, most notably Rudy Giuliani, who called for "trial by combat," hundreds of those who had attended the rally streamed toward the Capitol and soon turned into an angry mob.

By force of numbers, this mob breached the security of the Capitol. Some members of the mob ransacked offices. Others entered the chamber in which both the House and Senate were meeting and eventually resumed to meet once order was restored. Some even called for Pence to be lynched. In condemning this action, the nation not only condemned the violence and the interference with the function of government that it wrought, it also condemned the threat that the mob had posed to democracy itself. The mob sought to prevent Congress, required on that very day to receive and acknowledge the votes of the Electoral College, from giving effect to the outcome of the election of November 2020 and in that way from honoring the democratic aspirations of the Constitution.

THE ADVANCEMENT OF DEMOCRACY DURING THE CIVIL RIGHTS ERA

The violent assault on the Capitol on January 6, 2021, and the threat to interfere with the discharge of Congress's duty endows the events that occurred on that day with a certain singularity. Yet the more general threat that those events posed to the democratic aspirations of the Constitution has occurred on many occasions throughout American history. Sometimes would be voters were threatened with violence or economic coercion, often with the complicity of state law enforcement officers. Sometimes state legislative assemblies or state constitutional conventions devised ingenious ways of keeping countless citizens from voting and in so doing rendered various constitutional provisions, most blatantly the Fifteenth Amendment, a nullity. Adopted in 1870, that amendment sought to extend the purposes of the Thirteenth and Fourteenth Amendments and to provide additional constitutional support for the Reconstruction of the former slave states that was then afoot. In 1877, not long after the adoption of the Fifteenth Amendment, the federal government abandoned its commitment to Reconstruction and allowed the states to institutionalize practices that systematically denied countless Black citizens the right to vote. This blight on the Constitution endured for generations.

In May 1954, the Supreme Court began a new era in American history—some called it the Second Reconstruction—when, in *Brown v. Board of Education*, the Court repudiated the "separate but equal" doctrine that had governed since the nineteenth century.[7] In that decision, the Court condemned the Jim Crow school system and the racial caste system that it nourished and reinforced. In the wake of the *Brown* decision, social activists, particularly those representing the Student Nonviolent Coordinating Committee, brought increasing attention to the massive disenfranchisement of Blacks in the former states of the Confederacy. At the same time, Congress lent an arm to this historic endeavor and authorized the Attorney General to bring lawsuits to vindicate the right to vote. In the early 1960s, the Kennedy administration responded to this invitation and launched an ambitious litigation program to make the Fifteenth Amendment a living truth.[8]

In March 1965, state police brutally suppressed a march by civil rights activists in Selma, Alabama, demanding the right to vote, and the scenes of that violence were broadcast on television and covered by national newspapers. The nation was mobilized and within weeks Congress, thanks in part to the leadership of President Lyndon B. Johnson, passed the Voting Rights Act of 1965. This law banned many of the tests and devices that had been used for decades to block Blacks from voting and authorized the appointment, in special circumstances, of federal officials to register persons to vote. The 1965 act also required a select group of states and other political subdivisions—presumably the worst offenders—to submit, before they could go into effect, proposed changes in their election laws for approval to the Attorney General or a three-judge federal district court in Washington, DC. On signing it, President Johnson described the Voting Rights Act of 1965 as a "triumph for freedom as huge as any victory that has ever been won on any battlefield."[9]

During this same period of history, the federal judiciary played a key role in the progressive realization of the democratic ideal and its covenant with freedom. In the early 1960s, the federal judiciary handed down many decisions to redeem the promise of the Fifteenth Amendment. It documented, in precise and sometimes painful detail, the gross violations of that law and provided remedies to correct the wrong. The federal judiciary also swiftly and generously endorsed the congressional measures seeking to protect the right to vote. In that spirit, the Supreme Court handed down its ruling in *South Carolina v. Katzenbach*, which sustained the Voting Rights Act of 1965 in all its particulars.[10] Chief Justice Earl Warren wrote the opinion of the Court, as he had in *Brown v. Board of Education*. In writing his opinion in *South Carolina v. Katzenbach*, Warren used the authority of the Court to vindicate the right to vote and, in so doing, made the coordination, as opposed to the separation, of powers, a hallmark of the Second Reconstruction.

During the same era, the Court went out on its own, and by protecting the right to vote deepened our commitment to democracy. This occurred most notably in *Reynolds v. Sims*[11] and in *Harper v. Virginia Board of Elections*,[12] both of which were based on the

Equal Protection Clause of the Fourteenth Amendment. In *Reynolds*, also written by Warren and reportedly touted by him as his most important achievement, the Court rejected the apportionment of the Alabama legislature in the name of protecting the right to vote from dilution. In *Harper*, the Court, in an opinion by William Douglas, denied the states the power to make the payment of a tax, including a poll tax, a condition of voting. The Twenty-Fourth Amendment, adopted in 1964, denied states the power to make payment of a tax a condition of voting in elections choosing federal officials. The only question that remained following the adoption of that amendment was whether the same rule should apply to elections choosing state officials. In *Harper*, the Supreme Court held that it must.

Although *Reynolds* and *Harper* were decided almost at the same time as *South Carolina v. Katzenbach*, there was an important difference between these decisions. In *South Carolina v. Katzenbach*, the Court endorsed the work of Congress, a democratically constituted agency of government. In *Reynolds* and *Harper*, in contrast, the Court set aside the work of democratically constituted institutions, in these instances state legislatures, and in so doing created something of a paradox. The least democratic branch of government was setting aside, in the name of democracy, the work of elected branches of government, specifically the legislatures of the states. The issue was not confined to these two cases, in and of themselves, but rather extended to the entire legal tradition they spawned and came to represent.

In the case of *Reynolds v. Sims*, the paradox was partially obscured by the fact that the grossly malapportioned character of the Alabama legislature deprived that institution of the prerogatives ordinarily belonging to democratic institutions. Yet the Court's decision in *Reynolds v. Sims* did not stop at condemning the failure of the Alabama legislature to adjust the boundaries of electoral districts in a way that kept up with population shifts that occurred over a period of more than fifty years. It also affirmatively set the standard that the Alabama legislature, indeed all the state legislatures in the nation, had to meet when determining the bounds of electoral districts. Only months before, the Court in another case issued a similar requirement for congressional districts, which, according to the Constitution, were also to be drawn by state legislatures.[13]

In *Reynolds v. Sims*, the Court required all the electoral districts to contain approximately the same number of people and specifically denied the states the power to sacrifice this requirement in the effort to give greater representation to political subdivisions or to make any significant adjustments to render the electoral districts geographically compact. It may well seem odd that this rule, justified as a requirement of democracy and a protection of the right to vote, was thus promulgated by the Court, a non-democratic, in fact the least democratic branch of the national government. The same might be said, even more clearly, of the Court's decision in *Harper v. Virginia Board of Elections*, in which the Court set aside a statute of Virginia. In that case the Court denied the legislature the authority to condition voting on the payment of any tax, including a poll tax, even if that requirement were premised on the belief that the payment of taxes would help ensure the civic-mindedness of would-be voters.

Admittedly, the Supreme Court's power, as manifested in these decisions and others that built upon them, is not without democratic inflection. The President nominates the persons who become federal judges and these nominations must be confirmed by the Senate. It is also true that the jurisdiction of the federal courts, including that of the Supreme Court, is largely in the hands of Congress. In addition, the legislature may revise interpretations of a federal statute by the judiciary that it believes are mistaken or, under modern conditions, inappropriate. Congress need only pass a new statute.

Although these checks are of significance, in truth they mark the end of popular control. Although the interpretations of the

Constitution by the federal judiciary might be revised by constitutional amendment, the amendment process prescribed in the Constitution does not provide a significant opening for popular control. Some provisions, such as the rule requiring equal suffrage for the states in the Senate, are deemed unamendable. Even beyond that particular limitation, the amendment process is extremely cumbersome and grossly at variance with the democratic norm of requiring equality of votes. Under Article V, a coalition of the least populous states can block the adoption of an amendment favored by a majority of the American people. Moreover, in all cases, including constitutional ones, the judiciary, especially the federal judiciary and the Supreme Court, looks to the law—seen as an autonomous body of principles—not to the supposed will of the American people or the announced wishes of their elected officials.

In *Harper* and *Reynolds*, the Court was seeking to give concrete expression to the values embodied in the Constitution. In these two rulings, the Court was acting in much the same way as it did in *Brown v. Board of Education* and, for that matter, in *New York Times v. Sullivan*[14] and *Gideon v. Wainwright*,[15] to name only three landmark rulings in the period of Supreme Court history to which *Reynolds* and *Harper* belong. In *Brown*, the Court sought to give concrete meaning and expression to the promise of equal protection and did so by condemning the Jim Crow school system. In *Sullivan*, the Court was trying to give meaning to freedom of speech by putting limits on state defamation laws that might have the effect of insulating public officials from public criticism. In *Gideon*, the Court sought to give expression to the notion that defendants in criminal proceedings are entitled to the assistance of counsel and, in so doing, required the state to appoint and pay lawyers to represent those defendants who were indigent. Similarly, in *Reynolds* and *Harper*, the Court sought to give concrete meaning and expression to a constitutional value, specifically the commitment to democracy and the right to vote that it necessarily implies.

We can thus see that the paradox that we sought to explain—having the least democratic branch protect democracy—stems from the essential fact that the democracy we seek is a constitutional democracy. Our democratic aspirations are embodied in the Constitution and are thus properly advanced and protected by a court of law, even though that agency is not a democratic institution, nor even claims that it is. Grounding democracy in the basic charter of the nation adopted in 1787 and then extending that aspiration through a number of amendments enhances its future. It enables the proponents of democracy to summon the support of those who respect the rule of law. It also imposes upon a prominent and powerful social institution, namely the Supreme Court, the duty to watch over it—and, if need be, to protect freedom from itself.

Every elected official has the responsibility to respect the Constitution and thus to construe it. Every conscientious legislator, state or federal, must make a judgment whether the measure before the body is a valid exercise of the legislature's authority under the Constitution. The Constitution is the supreme law of the land. We count on the courts, however, to listen to those who are prepared to contest the understanding expressed by elected officials and then to resolve the merits of the dispute. The authority of the Supreme Court to have, so to speak, the last word on the Constitution stems from the allocation of power provided by Article III of the Constitution, not as a purely formal matter but rather as a reflection of the special procedural rules that have long controlled and still control the exercise of judicial power in common law countries. These rules require that judges be insulated from partisan politics and oblige them to hear from all aggrieved parties. They also require that judicial rulings and the trials that lead to them be held in public and that judges justify their rulings on the basis of public principles.

The Supreme Court is, as Ronald Dworkin once put it, "the forum of principle."[16]

VOTING AS A FUNDAMENTAL RIGHT

We have long counted on the federal judiciary and the Supreme Court in particular to give meaning and expression to the public values embodied in the Constitution, which I maintain includes the commitment to democracy and the right it necessarily implies—the right to vote. Starting in the 1960s, the Supreme Court has referred to the right to vote as precious or fundamental and that characterization of the right to vote has become one of the defining features of a constitutional tradition that is rooted in the Civil Rights Era and in *Reynolds v. Sims* as well as *Harper v. Virginia Board of Elections* in particular.

In *Reynolds*, the Court condemned Alabama's electoral districting scheme because the districts contained significant disparities in population and thus debased, diluted, and undervalued the votes of those living in the most populous districts. In that case, Chief Justice Earl Warren, writing for the majority, began his analysis by proclaiming: "No right is more precious in a free country than that of having a voice in the election of those who make the laws under which, as good citizens, we must live."[17] Justice William Douglas, who wrote the opinion for the Court in *Harper*, built on this very same understanding of the importance of the right to vote. He concluded his opinion on this note: "[W]ealth or fee paying has, in our view, no relation to voting qualifications; the right to vote is too precious, too fundamental to be so burdened or conditioned."[18]

Viewed from the perspective of individuals and a concern for their well-being, the claim about the special preciousness of the right to vote seems strained. It is hard to believe that, for the individual who is concerned with his or her welfare, the right to vote is more valuable or more precious than a right to a job, to food and housing, to education, to speak, or to worship. However, to more fully understand Warren and Douglas and the many other judges who spoke of the preciousness or fundamentality of the right to vote, we need to shift our focus.

We should not view this characterization of the importance of the right to vote from the perspective of the individual and his or her pragmatic interests. Rather, we must view the right to vote from a systemic perspective. We must understand that, in speaking about the preciousness or fundamentality of the right to vote, the justices were referring to the importance of that right in the system of government that the Constitution establishes, not to the welfare of individual voters. By protecting the right to vote, the Court, in cases such as *Reynolds*, *Harper*, and those that followed their lead, is doing more than protecting the pragmatic interest of each citizen. The Court is protecting democracy and the political freedom to which it gives rise.

The legal tradition rooted in *Reynolds v. Sims* and *Harper v. Virginia Board of Elections* is not only based on an understanding of the importance of the right to vote to the system of government. It is also premised on a unitary conception of the right—it must be as honored in the processes by which state officials are chosen as it is in the processes that select federal officials. Although as a federal union, citizens of the United States are subject to two types of rulers, those who belong to the national government and those who belong to the states, the constitutional promise of political freedom knows no such division. A people who would be able to choose one set of rulers but not the other would not be a free people. As a result, to achieve the freedom that democracy generates, the constitutional norms governing that ideal must be as applicable to the process by which state officials are chosen as they are to the processes by which federal officials are chosen. When it comes to democracy and the protection of the right to vote, the nation speaks with one voice. Not only is the right to vote precious or fundamental, it is also supremely national in character.

Under the terms of the Constitution, the states play a vital role in the election of federal officials—the 585 members of the House of Representatives, 100 senators, and the President and Vice President of the United States. The states initially set the qualifications for voting, manage the logistics of the process of voting, determine who should appear on the ballot, and define the boundaries of the congressional electoral districts (when their population allows for more than one member of the House of Representatives). In assigning these responsibilities to the states, the framers of the Constitution were either trying to avoid conflicts over slavery or other fundamental divisions prevalent at that time or, more modestly, trying to establish a workable and prudent scheme for the administration of elections over a large territory, one that would become even larger over time. The national interest in these exercises of state power over the election of federal officials is manifest and, like any other exercise of state power, these laws are subject to review by the federal judiciary, now to determine whether the state law has afforded sufficient respect to the right to vote, given its preciousness or fundamentality.

The national interest in the exercise of state power over the choice of state officials is less obvious, though equally vital. The freedom generated by the democratic selection of federal officials would mean nothing or little if state officials were chosen by nondemocratic processes or by processes that did not fully respect the elementary standards that govern the elections of federal officials. It would be like adding drops of ink to a glass of water—the color of the water would soon change. The American people would not be free.

Such a fear might well account for Article IV, Section 4 in the 1787 Constitution, which, as I noted before, provides that "the United

States shall guarantee to Every State in this Union a Republican Form of Government." A long line of cases assigns to Congress as opposed to the federal judiciary the responsibility for enforcing Section 4 of Article IV and that responsibility has been, for the most part, discharged in the process of admitting new states to the union. Even if these precedents are respected, however, we can see within Article IV a recognition of the national interest in the quality of state electoral processes and the importance of protecting the right to vote in elections for choosing state officials.

Article IV requires the United States to ensure a republican, not a democratic form of government. In a republic, as in a democracy, those who are ruled are given a right to choose their rulers, though the conception of the electorate might be narrower than the one that governs a democracy. A republic, as some of the delegates of the Philadelphia Convention envisioned, might even tolerate the exclusion of women and slaves from the electorate. Still, in a republic as in a democracy, power is vested in the people to choose their rulers. As Justice Douglas explained, in his 1962 concurrence in *Baker v. Carr*, "the right to vote is inherent in the republican form of government envisaged by Article IV."[19] This view is in accord with the framers' original understanding. In October 1787, only a month after the draft of the Constitution was sent to the states for ratification, James Madison wrote to Thomas Jefferson to explain that "the republican principle . . . refers the ultimate decision to the will of the majority." A few years later, James Wilson, in his concurrence in *Chisholm v. Georgia*, wrote: "My short definition of . . . a [republican] Government is, one constructed on the principle, that the Supreme Power resides in the body of the people."[20]

We can thus see in Article IV a recognition of the national interest in elections choosing state officials and this understanding is analogous, in both method and result, to the long-established process of incorporating and making applicable to the states certain enumerated rights found in the Bill of Rights. Consider, for example, the rule making the right to the assistance of counsel as applicable to state criminal trials as it is to federal criminal trials. Admittedly, the Court based the decision to incorporate the enumerated rights on the Due Process Clause of the Fourteenth Amendment. In truth, however, the Court was driven in this process of incorporation not by the text or any special history of the Fourteenth Amendment. Rather, the Court was recognizing the importance of state practices (such as criminal trials) in the ordinary life of citizens and the need to forge a single national identity with respect to the core freedoms that were enumerated in the Bill of Rights.

The need for a judicial judgment about the special importance of a right in the life of a nation is all the more clear when we acknowledge the selectivity of incorporation—the Court incorporated the right to the assistance of counsel, but not the right to a grand jury indictment. Consider also the rule in *Bolling v. Sharpe*, which in effect incorporated the Equal Protection Clause of the Fourteenth Amendment and made it applicable to the federal government.[21] As the Court explained in *Bolling*, any other result would be "unthinkable."[22] Viewed from this perspective, the national character of the right to vote and the rule making it govern the choice of state officials, though not an enumerated but rather a systemic right, is all the more compelling. It too depends on a judgment, this time about the unitary character of the political freedom that democracy promises and the importance of that freedom in defining the distinctive identity of the United States. We would not be a free people if we were only allowed to choose federal officials.

The Twenty-Fourth Amendment, adopted in January 1964 and which regulates the poll tax, might be read to reflect a contrary perspective. That amendment prohibits states from making the payment of a poll tax a qualification for voting but only does so in a limited way. It draws a distinction between the election of federal officials and the election of state officials and bans the payment of a poll tax for the election of the President and Vice President and the members of Congress. This feature of the Twenty-Fourth Amendment, however, is attributable to the special dynamics of the amendment process and to the political power that was wielded in the early 1960s by the so called Dixiecrats—Democratic senators from the southern states who openly resisted the advancement of civil rights. The limited reach of the amendment—making it applicable only to the election of federal officials—was needed to secure its ratification and does not represent a statement about the reach or importance of the democratic mandate of the Constitution or the freedom it generates. In 1966, only two years after the adoption of that amendment, the Supreme Court reaffirmed the reach of that mandate—we speak as one nation—when it banned in *Harper v. Virginia Board of Elections* the payment of the poll tax as a qualification for voting for state officials in much the same way as the Twenty-Fourth Amendment had banned it for the election of federal officials.

In *Reynolds v. Sims*, Warren spoke in broad terms, honoring the unity of political freedom. He said, "Undeniably the Constitution of the United States protects the right of all qualified citizens to vote, in state as well as in federal elections."[23] Douglas proceeded more cautiously in *Harper v. Virginia Board of Elections*, either because the case put into issue what Warren assumed (the qualifications of the would-be voters) or because he wrote in the shadow of the Twenty-Fourth Amendment. In *Harper*, Douglas acknowledged that the Court had upheld, at least since the 1940s, the existence of the right to vote in the elections of federal officials, but then invoked the Equal Protection Clause in such a way as to avoid resolving the question of whether there was a federal constitutional right to vote in elections of state officers. According to Douglas, counsel for the would-be voters argued that the right to vote in these elections might be "implicit, particularly by reason of the First Amendment."[24] But then Douglas immediately responded: "We do not stop to canvass the relationship between voting and political expression. For it is enough to say that once the franchise is granted to the electorate, lines may not be drawn which are inconsistent with the Equal Protection Clause of the Fourteenth Amendment."[25]

At the time *Harper* was decided, the antidiscrimination principle controlled equal protection jurisprudence. Under this principle, the Equal Protection Clause was seen primarily as a ban on racial discrimination when, for example, the state assigned students among schools or allocated scarce opportunities such as jobs. Douglas paid homage to this understanding of equal protection when, in *Harper v. Virginia Board of Elections*, he condemned the poll tax as a form of wealth discrimination. He reasoned that wealth would be as impermissible a basis as race for allocating a scarce opportunity or for selectively distributing the franchise. In truth, however, the poll tax did not discriminate on the basis of wealth. Everyone, rich or poor, had to pay the tax. Of course, paying the poll tax was a greater burden for the poor to pay than it would be for a rich person. Or, to put it in more modern terms, a flat tax on everyone had an adverse, disparate impact on the poor. Such a disparate impact would be present whenever the state charged a fee—tuition for a state university, bus fare, or even, to mention the example that especially fascinated Douglas, for obtaining a driver's license. There was, however, no indication that the Court or even a slim majority was then prepared to condemn all these fees as a denial of equal protection. The need for a limiting principle was manifest.

In the end, Douglas found that principle in the specialness of voting—that the right to vote, even in an election choosing state officials, was precious or fundamental. Recall that he ended his opinion on this note: "The right to vote is too precious, too fundamental, to be so burdened or conditioned." Yet to fall back on the fundamentality or preciousness of the right to vote in a state election makes equal protection as the ground of the decision superfluous or redundant. Any interference with or burden placed on the exercise of a fundamental or precious right would be condemned, not as a breach of equal protection but rather as a breach of the constitutional norm making that right fundamental—in our case, democracy. In sum, although Douglas invoked equal protection and the prohibition on wealth discrimination to avoid deciding whether there was a federal constitutional right to vote in elections choosing state officials, in order to make that argument work, he had to assume the existence of that right—the right to vote. He had to posit that which he sought to avoid.

The weakness of the wealth discrimination theory in *Harper* was, I venture to say, even grasped by Douglas himself. As I noted, at the outset of his analysis, Douglas made a distinction between the right to vote in elections choosing federal officials and those choosing state officials. He noted that the Court in the 1941 decision *United States v. Classic* already decided that there was a federal constitutional right to vote in elections choosing federal officials that arose from Article I, Section 2. He then claimed that it was unnecessary to decide, as counsel argued, whether there was a federal constitutional right to vote in elections choosing state officials. According to Douglas, the availability of the Equal Protection Clause, which unquestionably governs the election of state officials, made it unnecessary for him to resolve the argument by counsel for the would-be voter, which, as Douglas saw it, seemed to use the First Amendment as the basis for implying the right to vote in elections choosing state officials.

At that very point in his opinion, Douglas, in an obvious gesture of admiration, inserted a footnote reporting on a recent ruling by a three-judge court invalidating a Texas poll tax. The whole of the footnote reads:

Judge Thornberry, speaking for the three-judge court which recently declared the Texas poll tax unconstitutional, said: "If the state of Texas placed a tax on the right to speak at the rate of one dollar and seventy-five cents per year, no court would hesitate to strike it down as a blatant infringement of the freedom of speech. Yet the poll tax as enforced in Texas is a tax on the equally important right to vote."[26]

Note that Thornberry did not make the right to vote an appendix to the right to speak nor did he use the First Amendment as the source or basis of implying the right to vote. Rather, he said only that the right to vote was equally important. If you cannot be required to pay a fee for speaking, you should not be able to require a fee for voting.

On this reading, the right vindicated by *Harper* is the right to vote, not the right to equal protection. An interference with or burden on the exercise of the right to vote is not a trigger of strict scrutiny (the test governing the Equal Protection Clause) but a violation of the right itself, derived, as it is, from the democratic purposes of the Constitution taken as a whole. Voting is the essential process through which a people are rendered free—those who are ruled choose their rulers. For that reason, voting should not be dependent on the resources citizens have or on their willingness to expend these resources to be able to participate in this process.

The footnote on Thornberry's ruling also helps us understand the need to maintain the unity of the political freedom that democracy generates and why *Harper*'s prohibition on making the payment of a poll tax or for that matter any tax a condition of voting must be made applicable to all the elections administered by Virginia. We, as a nation, can only enjoy the freedom democracy promises if the federal constitutional right to vote covers both types of elections, those in which state officials are chosen as well as those in which federal officials are chosen. The right to vote emanating from the national constitution is a national right, much like the right guaranteeing freedom of speech.

In trying to maintain the necessary unity of political freedom, *Harper* appeared in tension with the distinction that the Twenty-Fourth Amendment drew between the election of federal officials versus the election of state officials. Yet that decision was very much in accord with Section 2 of the Fourteenth Amendment as well as the Fifteenth and Nineteenth Amendments. These provisions govern the elections of both state and federal officials. Moreover, in 1971, soon after *Harper* was handed down, the Twenty-Sixth Amendment decreed that the right to vote of citizens of the United States who are eighteen or older shall not be denied or abridged by the United States or any state on account of age. In giving the right to vote this broad, undifferentiated scope, the Constitution, once again, proclaimed the unity of political freedom.

CHAPTER 2

. . .

Extending the Franchise

MANY FACTORS MAY be responsible for the gradual extension of the franchise that has occurred in the United States over the course of the nation's history: the quest for partisan advantage; the view that certain long-excluded groups are as entitled to vote as everyone else; and the hope that giving the vote to long-disadvantaged groups would, in and of itself, improve their status. In addition to these dynamics, however, I also maintain that this process of extending the franchise may be attributable to the inner logic of democracy. The freedom that democracy promises arises only when those who are ruled are allowed to elect their leaders, and thus democracy itself, as a guiding principle of the Constitution, creates a dynamic that leans toward extending the franchise to all who are ruled. Democracy embodies a principle that I, following Cara Meyer, call the requirement of coextensionality. It provides that those who are ruled must be allowed to vote.

Several amendments to the Constitution beginning with the Fourteenth and Fifteenth Amendments, both adopted immediately after the end of the Civil War, give powerful expression to this

Why We Vote. Owen Fiss, Oxford University Press. © Owen Fiss 2024.
DOI: 10.1093/oso/9780197746387.003.0003

principle of coextensionality. The Fourteenth Amendment provided the newly freed slaves with United States citizenship when it stipulated that all persons born within the United States and subject to its jurisdiction are citizens of the United States and then conferred upon them the privileges and immunities of citizens of the United States. Section 2 of that amendment specified the penalty for disenfranchisement—a reduction of representation of the state responsible for it—and in so doing spoke of "the right to vote," and, as stressed in Chapter 1, made it clear that this right extends to the elections of both state and federal officials. Two years later, in 1870, the Fifteenth Amendment affirmed and strengthened this democratic promise. The Fifteenth Amendment specifically provided that the right to vote shall not be denied on the basis of race or previous condition of servitude. It also authorized Congress to enact measures to enforce this prohibition. Unlike Section 2 of the Fourteenth Amendment, the Fifteenth Amendment did not specify a remedy for the violation of the general mandate. It assumed that the judiciary, when implementing Section 1, would fashion its remedy, typically an injunction setting aside the state law or practice that it determined interfered with the right to vote.

The Nineteenth Amendment, adopted in 1920, extended the franchise to women, and thus gave forceful, indeed monumental, expression to the democratic ideal and its requirement of coextensionality. This amendment in effect doubled the number of voters. The Twenty-Sixth Amendment, adopted in 1971, in the middle of the Vietnam War, also broadened the franchise by lowering the voting age to eighteen. The sponsors of this amendment were mindful that any man could be drafted and thus be required to put his life on the line when he turned eighteen. If, as the sponsors reasoned, a person is old enough to be drafted, he should be deemed old enough to vote. Admittedly, implicit in the Twenty-Sixth Amendment is a permission for the states to deny the right to vote to any person under eighteen—children. Such an exclusion can only be reconciled with the requirement of coextensionality by a theory of virtual representation, which postulates that the interests and wishes of children are represented by their parents. Such a theory of representation is strictly limited by the unique relation that exists between parents and children.

On occasion, the institutions of the federal government, including the political branches, have played a vital role in extending the franchise and implementing the democratic requirement of coextensionality. The most remarkable achievement in this regard consists of the Voting Rights Act of 1965. It eliminated a wide variety of tests and devices, such as literacy tests, that had been used to exclude Blacks from the polls and to render the right to vote granted by the Fourteenth and Fifteenth Amendments a hollow promise. In enacting the Voting Rights Act, Congress did not purport to outlaw these tests as an abstract matter nor deem them inconsistent on their face with democracy. Instead, Congress relied on the elaborate findings entered by the federal judiciary, supplemented by legislative inquiries, that demonstrated that state and local officials systematically used their discretion inherent in such tests to prevent Blacks from voting.

Later, in 1969, the Supreme Court upheld a ban on literacy tests on the theory that they extended and perpetuated the discrimination inflicted on Blacks through a system of public education governed by Jim Crow.[1] This occurred in a case that had come to the Court through the preclearance procedure instituted by the Voting Rights Act. That procedure required a select number of jurisdictions—the most flagrant and persistent violators of the Fourteenth and Fifteenth Amendments—to seek review, by either the Attorney General or a three-judge court sitting in Washington, of any new law affecting the right to vote. In 2013, the Supreme Court issued a ruling in *Shelby County v. Holder* that had the effect of rendering this form of preventive relief inoperative.[2] The Court ruled that the formula that Congress had used to determine which jurisdictions were in fact subject to preclearance review had become anachronistic and ill-fitting because the formula included some jurisdictions whose records were better than those omitted. The Court did not strike down the general idea of preclearance nor did it lessen in any way the ban on tests or devices such as literacy tests, either because of the discretion that they vested in local officials or because they perpetuated the disadvantages imposed by the public education system.

In the very same era in which the Voting Rights Act of 1965 was enacted, and arguably in response to the very same pressures that moved Congress and the President, the Supreme Court also played a crucial role in extending the franchise and honoring the principle of coextensionality. The Court warmly and immediately embraced the 1965 Voting Rights Act, deeming that statute a proper exercise of the powers Congress possessed under the provisions of the Fourteenth and Fifteenth Amendments, giving congressional authority to enforce the general prohibitions of these amendments. The Court also went one step further. It invalidated state laws that established qualifications to vote. The Court did not declare these state laws inconsistent with democracy, seen as a guiding ideal of the Constitution, nor did it declare the state law invalid because the law degraded the constitutionally protected right to vote. Rather, the Court concluded that the state laws imposing the qualifications on voting violated the provision of the Fourteenth Amendment guaranteeing equal protection of the law.

In these cases, the Court held that every state law establishing qualifications for the franchise was to be judged by the strict scrutiny test. A state law that denied some the right to vote would be set aside unless the state could show that the law was necessary for securing some compelling public purpose. The very idea of strict scrutiny can be traced back to the 1940s when Justice Hugo Black, writing for the Court in the *Japanese Relocation Cases*, indicated that the practice of using racial classification should be subject to especially strict scrutiny.[3] *Brown v. Board of Education* did not use the strict scrutiny test in any way; the Court's judgment was instead based on the view that Jim Crow education impaired the equality of educational opportunity required by the Equal Protection Clause. However, in the course of the 1960s, as the momentum to desegregate schools gained traction and the legitimacy of the *Brown* decision was more firmly established, the rule requiring a strict or exacting scrutiny test of state laws embodying a racial classification became increasingly entrenched. As this occurred, the Court developed yet another strand of strict scrutiny, this time for state laws that interfered with or burdened the exercise of what was deemed a fundamental right.

The category of fundamental rights was not self-limiting, though during the 1960s it was assumed, on the bench and in political circles, that the right to vote was a fundamental right. Indeed, many saw the right to vote as the paradigmatic fundamental right. As a result, the Equal Protection Clause, now governed by strict scrutiny, became an effective, though oblique instrument for implementing the coextensionality requirement and the democratic purpose of the Constitution. The right to vote was not treated as an independent basis of the Court's decision, but only as a trigger of strict scrutiny requiring, as when the state employed a racial classification, that the state show that any law denying a group of persons the right to vote was necessary to achieve a compelling public purpose.

In *Harper v. Virginia Board of Elections*, handed down in 1966, the Supreme Court invalidated a state law that established the payment of a poll tax as a condition of exercising the right to vote, and in that way honored the coextensionality principle of democracy. Justice Douglas wrote the Court's opinion, but the role in his thinking of this new branch of strict scrutiny—the one protecting fundamental

[33]

rights—was not at all clear. Thanks to his experience in resisting the anti-communist crusade of the McCarthy era, Douglas was distrustful of any balancing test. He therefore was no friend of strict scrutiny, which he viewed as nothing more than another balancing test.[4] His antipathy toward balancing and strict scrutiny was forged in First Amendment cases, and yet it presumably governed his understanding of the Fourteenth Amendment as well. For that reason, he did not, in so many words, apply the fundamental rights branch of strict scrutiny in *Harper*, although his words might be read as implicitly applying such a test. Recall that he declared, for reasons described in Chapter 1, that the right to vote was "precious" or "fundamental" and then concluded his opinion on this note: "Wealth or fee paying has, in our view, no relation to voting qualifications; the right to vote is too precious, too fundamental to be so burdened or conditioned."[5]

Chief Justice Warren, the author of *Reynolds v. Sims*, did not share Douglas's reluctance to use the fundamental rights branch of strict scrutiny. In *Kramer v. Union Free School District No. 15*, handed down in 1969 shortly before his retirement, Warren openly employed the fundamental rights branch of strict scrutiny and did so in a case with no racial overtones.[6] Speaking for the Court, Warren struck down a New York statute, primarily applicable to suburban and rural school districts, that limited the right to vote in school board elections to persons who owned or leased taxable property in the school district, or who were parents or guardians of children enrolled in the public schools. In the opinion for the Court, Warren insisted that any state law that selectively distributes the franchise must be subject to the most exacting scrutiny. The Court was required, Warren thought, to make certain that the public purposes allegedly served by the law—in this instance, confining the vote to those primarily interested in school affairs—were compelling and furthermore that the means the New York legislature used to achieve that purpose were narrowly tailored.

Applying this test, Warren carefully listed the residents in the district who would be denied the vote under the New York law. The list included those without children in school who neither owned nor leased taxable property; clergy and military who lived on tax exempt property and had no children in school; senior citizens living with relatives; boarders or lodgers; and all parents who neither owned nor leased property in the district and whose children either went to private schools or were too young to attend public school. Many of these people, Warren reasoned, were as interested in the quality and structure of public education as those who were given the franchise, and from this misfit between means and ends, he concluded that the law was invalid. At this point, it seemed as though the principle of coextensionality would be fully implemented and any state law limiting the allocation of the vote would be subject to exacting judicial review.

A NEW TURN IN THE LAW

The *Kramer* decision was announced on June 16, 1969. A week later, Warren retired. This retirement marked the beginning of a five-year period in which there was significant turnover in the personnel of the Court, and a new governing coalition emerged—one that had little taste for extending the right to vote or the implementation of the requirement I call coextensionality. The prerogative to fill the vacancies that occurred during this period fell to Richard Nixon, the Republican candidate who had won the 1968 election and who remained in the White House until August 1974, at which point he resigned to avoid impeachment.

During his tenure, President Nixon appointed to the Court Warren Burger, Harry Blackmun, Lewis Powell, and William Rehnquist. Burger was named Chief Justice. In the course of the 1968 campaign, Nixon ran against the Warren Court and, presumably, his nominations to the Court were in accord with his campaign promises. His criticism—sometimes in coded language—focused on school desegregation and the Court's effort to reform police practices. For obvious reasons, Nixon did not attack the landmark decisions of the Court such as *Reynolds v. Sims* and *Harper v. Virginia Board of Elections* that proclaimed the fundamentality of the right to vote and implemented the democratic ideal. Yet in time, the new appointees were responsible for decisions that limited and drained such decisions of their generative force.

The change did not come all at once—it never does. In 1972, the Court, in *Dunn v. Blumstein*, invalidated a Tennessee law that denied the franchise to anyone who had not resided in the state for a year.[7] Using the fundamental rights branch of strict scrutiny, the Court reasoned that whatever salutary purpose might be served by such a residency requirement—to prevent fraud, to assure familiarity with the candidates' position on contested issues, or to facilitate the registration process—could be satisfied by a thirty-day residency requirement. The attachment of President Nixon's appointees to this result or, even more, to the fundamental rights branch of strict scrutiny was not at all clear. Burger dissented. Blackmun, expressing unease with strict scrutiny, only concurred in the result. Powell and Rehnquist did not participate in the case, presumably because they had not yet taken their seats on the Court when the case was argued.[8]

In 1974, the newly constituted Court handed down *Richardson v. Ramirez*, and in that decision its hostility to the fundamental rights branch of strict scrutiny became abundantly clear.[9] The majority upheld a California law that denied the right to vote to ex-felons—citizens who had been convicted of a felony but whose sentence and time for parole or probation had ended. All four of the Nixon appointees were part of the majority, and they were able to garner the support of Potter Stewart and Byron White.

Although Stewart and White had served under Warren and joined the majority in *Dunn v. Blumstein*, their attachment to the jurisprudence of that era extending the franchise was limited. In fact, Stewart had dissented in *Kramer v. Union Free School District No. 15*, sharply opposing the extension of the strict scrutiny test from its original civil rights context and the transformation of it into an instrument for protecting the right to vote. White was no friend of strict scrutiny either.[10] To write the Court's opinion in *Richardson v. Ramirez*, Burger turned to Rehnquist, who played a key role in defining the agenda and doctrine of the new governing coalition.[11] In 1986, President Ronald Reagan, conforming outward appearances to the inner reality, elevated Rehnquist to become Chief Justice, and he served as Chief until his death in 2005.

The three stalwarts of the Warren Court who were sitting at the time of *Richardson v. Ramirez*, William Douglas, William Brennan, and Thurgood Marshall, all dissented. Douglas dissented on procedural grounds. He thought that the California Supreme Court, which had struck down the rule disenfranchising ex-felons, rested on an interpretation of California law and thus was under standard doctrine beyond the reach of federal courts. It did not matter, according to Douglas, that the California court's construction of state law was guided by federal precedents.

Brennan deferred to Marshall and allowed him to write the dissent, which he joined. After all, Marshall had written the Court's decision in *Dunn v. Blumstein*. Although Marshall, like Douglas, believed that there was an independent ground supporting the judgment below, he went on to consider the constitutionality of the California law denying ex-felons the right to vote. He understood the pragmatic significance of Rehnquist's opinion. It left millions of Americans—all ex-felons—without the right to vote. Marshall also grasped the large threat that Rehnquist's approach posed to the power of the Court to review state practices that limited the right to vote.

As he did in *Dunn v. Blumstein*, Marshall applied the fundamental rights branch of strict scrutiny, denying that the disenfranchisement of ex-felons was necessary for the achievement of any compelling state purpose. Such an exclusion, he argued, was "patently both overinclusive and underinclusive."[12] Although he viewed the prevention of electoral fraud as a compelling state interest, he maintained that there was no evidence that ex-felons were more likely to engage in electoral fraud than the rest of the population. He also noted that electoral fraud convictions were, under California law, classified as misdemeanors and thus not included in the class (ex-felons) that was in fact barred by California from voting. In addition, Marshall pointed to the elaborate provisions in the California criminal code that were designed to prevent electoral fraud. These provisions, according to Marshall, rendered the law denying the vote to ex-felons redundant or unnecessary—it thus failed the requirement that the least restrictive means be employed to further the alleged compelling state interest.

In this way, Marshall paid homage to the familiar terms of the fundamental rights branch of the strict scrutiny test, specifically to its narrow tailoring component that was so essential to *Kramer* and *Dunn*. Yet it should be noted that he also openly acknowledged the imperatives of the democratic ideal and the requirement of coextensionality (though he expressed it in more graceful terms) when he wrote: "There is certainly no basis for asserting that ex-felons have any less interest in the democratic process than any other citizen. Like everyone else, their daily lives are deeply affected and changed by the decisions of government." Marshall's thinking about the essentials of democracy became even clearer when he identified and then rejected what might, in addition to electoral fraud, be offered as a compelling state purpose for the exclusion of ex-felons—the fear of how ex-felons might vote. Marshall acknowledged that some may want to keep ex-felons from voting, "for fear that they might vote to repeal or emasculate provisions of the criminal code."[13] He refused, however, to accept the need to respond to that fear as a compelling state purpose, as strict scrutiny required. Indeed, Marshall would not even regard the need to respond to this fear as a permissible or legitimate state purpose. Honoring that fear, Marshall said, would defeat the very purpose of democracy, namely to allow those who are subjected to the laws to change them. To illustrate his argument, he made reference to the American experience with the prohibition of alcohol and, with a touch of prescience, he also made reference to debates over the legalization of marijuana. If, Marshall argued, we accept a fear of how ex-felons may use their vote, "those who support the legalization of marihuana could be barred from the ballot box."[14] For Marshall, "The process of democracy is one of change."[15]

It must be stressed that Rehnquist did not respond to Marshall's application of the strict scrutiny test or, even more, to the idea upon which it rested, namely that the right to vote is a fundamental or especially precious right. Rehnquist finessed the merits, so to speak, by reading Section 2 of the Fourteenth Amendment to deny ex-felons or anyone convicted of a crime the capacity to invoke, in an effort to gain the right to vote, the Equal Protection Clause or any other provision of Section 1 of the Fourteenth Amendment, including the guarantee to those born in the United States of the privileges and immunities of citizens of the United States. To fully understand Rehnquist's strategy, we must step back and take a look at Section 2 as a whole.

Section 2 has three distinct provisions. The first, accounting for the Thirteenth Amendment and the end of slavery, provides that the apportionment of representatives in the House among the states shall be based on the whole number of persons in each state. Previously only three-fifths of the number of slaves were counted for purposes of apportioning representatives. The second provision of Section 2 acknowledges or possibly even grants a right to vote in federal and state elections to those made citizens by Section 1 of the Fourteenth Amendment. This provision of Section 2 lists the elections to which the right is to be honored: "any election for the choice of electors for the President or Vice President of the United States, representatives in Congress, the Executive and Judicial offices of a State, or the members of the Legislature thereof." The third provision of Section 2 creates a sanction for denials or abridgements of the right to vote: the number of representatives apportioned to each state under the terms of the first provision shall be reduced in proportion to the number of persons who are denied the right to vote. Reflecting the norms prevailing in 1868, Section 2 makes it clear that the right to vote only extends to male citizens twenty-one years of age.

To calculate the reduction of representatives, Section 2 directs that the number of representatives shall be reduced by calculating the portion of eligible voters who are denied the right to vote compared to the total number of eligible voters. It then uses that proportion to reduce the number of representatives. So, if 10% of the male citizens over twenty-one years of age are denied the right to vote, then the population used for determining the number of representatives shall be reduced by 10%. Section 2 also provides—and here is, at least for Rehnquist, the kicker—that in calculating the number of male citizens above the age of twenty-one who are denied the right to vote, no account shall be taken of the number of persons who are in fact denied the vote because of "participation in rebellion, or other crime."

Rehnquist used this exclusion in the remedy specified in Section 2 to preclude or bar any consideration whatsoever of the claim that the California bar on ex-felons violated any of the broad, general guarantees of Section 1 of the Fourteenth Amendment. Marshall believed that Rehnquist was exaggerating the significance of the exclusion. He acknowledged that disenfranchisement of those convicted of crimes was common when the Fourteenth Amendment was adopted. Yet, taking his bearings from a decision he knew so well—*Brown v. Board of Education*—Marshall maintained that the prevalence of a state practice that was predominant at the time a decision was adopted did not prevent the Court from finding that practice a violation of Section 1.

Nor did Justice Marshall believe that the phrase "or other crime" in Section 2 created an exemption for the broad mandates of Section 1. It only required that, for purposes of applying the remedy stipulated in Section 2—a reduction of representation in the House—the count of the number of persons disenfranchised shall not include the number of persons who were disenfranchised because they had been convicted of a crime. This limitation on the Section 2 remedy should not exempt from review, Marshall maintained, any state law, even one denying the vote to persons convicted of a crime, from judicial review under Section 1. In such a case, the judiciary would have its own remedy, namely the invalidation of the state law.

Marshall viewed the phrase "or other crime" as nothing more than a limitation on the specific reduction-of-representation remedy of Section 2 and drew support for this view from the origins of Section 2. He explained that Section 2 went to the joint congressional committee responsible for drafting containing an exclusion only "for participation in rebellion" and, as he said, it "emerged with 'other crime' inexplicably tacked on." Rehnquist refused to confine the Section 2 exclusion for "other crime" in this way. He wrote: "It is as much a part of the [Fourteenth] Amendment as any of the other sections, and how it became a part of the Amendment is less important than what it says and what it means."

The meaning of Section 2 is far from clear. The exemption for "other crime" possibly includes conviction for the most trivial of crimes, such as traffic violations. Similarly, the consequences of the phrase "or other crime" is also unclear. Arguably, it might exempt the practice of disenfranchising those convicted of a crime from the reduction-of-representation remedy provided for in Section 2, but leave untouched the reach of the guarantees of Section 1. Although in 1974, in *Richardson v. Ramirez*, Rehnquist viewed it as applicable to any crime and then gave it preemptive effect over Section 1, a decade later—in *Hunter v. Underwood*, handed down in 1985, shortly before he was to be named Chief Justice by President Reagan— Rehnquist reversed himself.[16] Powell did not participate in that decision but all the other Justices, including Marshall and Brennan, joined Rehnquist's opinion.

Hunter did not involve the disenfranchisement of ex-felons. The suit challenging the state law was brought by two persons—one Black, the other white—who were denied the right to vote because they were each convicted of a misdemeanor, specifically, presenting a worthless check. The voting registrar who had denied these individuals the right to vote acted under a provision of the Alabama constitution, Section 182, that was adopted in the state constitutional convention of 1901.

In defining the scope of disenfranchisement, Section 182 listed a large number of offenses—treason, murder, arson, larceny, robbery, perjury, etc.—and then added two catch-alls: one for "any crime punishable by imprisonment" and a second for "any infamous crime or crime involving moral turpitude." Apparently, presenting a worthless check fell under the second catch-all, which was construed to embrace some (though not all) misdemeanors. The two persons barred from voting under Section 182 brought a class action in federal court and, in an opinion by Rehnquist, the Supreme Court held

Section 182 to be a violation of the Equal Protection Clause and thus unconstitutional on its face (that is, in all its possible applications). Shortly after *Richardson v. Ramirez* was decided, the Supreme Court handed down its decision in *Washington v. Davis*,[17] soon to be reaffirmed in *Arlington Heights*.[18] In those cases, the Court concluded that the Equal Protection Clause, on its own, did not bar state laws simply because they had an adverse disparate impact on Blacks. A discriminatory intent had to be shown. Proof was required that the law in question was adopted for the purpose of excluding or otherwise disadvantaging Blacks. In *Hunter v. Underwood*, Rehnquist concluded that the rule of *Washington v. Davis* and *Arlington Heights* was satisfied and for that purpose relied on the finding of the Court of Appeals, which had invalidated Section 182 because it had been adopted for the purpose of discriminating against all Blacks and that purpose was a "but-for" motivation for its enactment.[19]

The record indicated that the members of the 1901 convention that had adopted Section 182 understood that the law would disenfranchise poor whites as well as Blacks (all of whom were poor) and that such disenfranchisement was one of its purposes. Rehnquist ruled, however, that even if the disenfranchisement of poor whites was an "additional purpose" of the law, it "would not render nugatory the purpose to discriminate against all blacks," especially when the law also had a racial discriminatory impact.[20]

The plaintiffs in *Hunter v. Underwood* sought a judgment in the federal court against the application or enforcement of Section 182, not just a historical judgment about what transpired in the 1901 convention. Accordingly, the state maintained that regardless of the original purpose of Section 182, conviction of a crime, whether it be a felony or a misdemeanor involving moral turpitude (for example, issuing worthless checks) is an acceptable basis for denying the franchise. Rehnquist brusquely put that argument of the state aside in a single sentence. It read, "[w]ithout deciding whether § 182 would be valid if enacted today without any impermissible motivation, we simply observe that its original enactment was motivated by a desire to discriminate against blacks on account of race and the section continues to this day to have that effect."[21]

Then, in the final two sentences of his opinion, Rehnquist dealt with the issue central to his opinion in *Richardson v. Ramirez*, namely the preemptive effect of Section 2 of the Fourteenth Amendment on Section 1 of that amendment and, in particular, the Equal Protection Clause. In *Hunter v. Underwood*, Rehnquist simply said, "we are confident that § 2 was not designed to permit the purposeful racial discrimination attending the enactment and operation of § 182 [of the Alabama constitution] which otherwise violates § 1 of the Fourteenth Amendment."[22]

True, the disenfranchisement of ex-felons by the state of California in *Richardson v. Ramirez* was not attacked on the ground that it discriminated, in either purpose or effect, against Blacks. Yet the California law was attacked on another branch of equal protection, the one that allows the abridgement of a fundamental right (the right to vote) only if the law in question serves a compelling state purpose and is narrowly tailored to achieve that purpose. In that context, Rehnquist, speaking for a majority in *Richardson v. Ramirez*, ruled that Section 2 controls Section 1 and furthermore that Section 2 thus precludes any consideration of the merits of that constitutional claim. Section 2 was given, as I said, preemptive effect. The decision in *Hunter v. Underwood*, however, threw that ruling into doubt, unless some magical way can be found to read Section 2 to have preemptive effect over one type of equal protection claim (seeking to protect the exercise of a fundamental right) but not over another (to protect against racial discrimination). There is nothing, however, in the words or history of Section 2 that would permit such a bifurcation.

For that reason, I believe, the 1986 decision in *Hunter v. Underwood* created a new opening. While *Richardson v. Ramirez* had turned Section 2 into a rule blocking judicial examination under Section 1 of a state law disenfranchising persons who had been convicted of a felony, *Hunter v. Underwood* called that rule into question and did so despite Rehnquist's disclaimer. Yet *Richardson v. Ramirez* was not just a precedent; it was also a symbol. It signaled that, by 1974, a controlling bloc had coalesced on the Court dedicated to repudiating or at least limiting the doctrine announced by the Warren Court—the fundamental rights branch of strict scrutiny—that was aimed at extending the franchise to all who are ruled and thus at implementing the democratic ideal and its requirement of coextensionality. The new majority formed in 1974 did not openly repudiate the democratic aspiration of the Constitution, but dramatically lessened the tribunal's commitment to it.

Over the next half century, the bloc of Justices responsible for the 1974 ruling in *Richardson v. Ramirez* was replenished on a number of occasions, thanks to the appointments of a series of Republican presidents: Ronald Reagan (1981–1989), George H. Bush (1989–1993), George W. Bush (2001–2009), and Donald J. Trump (2017–2021). There was no appetite in this group of appointees, taken as a whole, to explore the democratic potential of *Hunter v. Underwood*. Although *Hunter* remained on the books, its reach was strictly limited to cases where the discriminatory purpose of the general rule disenfranchising a group defined in non-racial terms was manifest. The kind of evidence of discrimination that was evident in *Hunter* itself was lacking in most other disenfranchisement cases. At the same time, the rule of *Washington v. Davis* and *Arlington Heights*, denying the sufficiency of racially disparate impact to establish a violation of equal protection, became more deeply entrenched. Moreover, there was no inclination in this group of new appointees to revive the fundamental rights branch of strict scrutiny under equal protection.

Even after *Richardson v. Ramirez*, other avenues for reform and for honoring the requirement of coextensionality remained. The enforcement provisions of the Fourteenth and Fifteenth Amendments provide ample authority for Congress to extend the franchise to ex-felons. In 1966, the Supreme Court held that Congress could outlaw state practices under Section 5 of the Fourteenth Amendment that the Court itself had not deemed a violation of Section 1.[23] In later years, the Court circumscribed that interpretation of the enforcement clause of the Fourteenth Amendment by requiring that the congressional statute be congruent and proportional.[24] Even so, the power of Congress to ban a state practice that the Court had not deemed a violation of Section 1 remains, though protracted political divisions within Congress have made it unlikely that such a measure would be passed.

In some states, including California, popular repeal of state laws disenfranchising ex-felons has been notably successful. On the other hand, the Supreme Court has refused to lend any support to such endeavors. Worse yet, in 2020, the Court gave further life to *Richardson v. Ramirez*—looking to its spirit, rather than its letter—when it failed to protect a state-wide popular referendum in Florida extending the vote to ex-felons from being frustrated by the Florida legislature and Supreme Court of Florida. Both of President Barack Obama's appointments to the Supreme Court—Sonia Sotomayor (appointed in 2009) and Elena Kagan (appointed in 2010)—protested this stance of the Court and the breach of the requirement of coextensionality.

In 2018, the voters of Florida had sought to give expression to the principle of coextensionality. They amended the state constitution to provide: "any disqualification from voting arising from a felony conviction shall terminate and voting rights shall be restored upon completion of all terms of sentence, including parole or probation." An exception was made for those convicted of murder or a sex offense. The Florida legislature, responding to a call from the governor, Ron DeSantis, construed the amendment to impose yet another barrier to the enfranchisement of ex-felons within the state. The legislature decreed that those seeking the benefit of the constitutional amendment, in addition to serving their prescribed time in prison and the termination of their terms of probation or parole, would have to pay certain financial obligations imposed on them. Specifically, they would have to pay all the court fees and costs, fines levied as part of the sentence, and the restitution to the victim that might have been part of their sentence. This barrier to voting was later confirmed by an advisory opinion of the Supreme Court of Florida, sought by the governor. The Florida court concluded that the legislature had correctly interpreted the phrase "all terms."

A familiar rule of federal jurisprudence allows state courts to be the arbiter of state law. But exceptions have been recognized when the interpretation jeopardizes a national right and appears, on its face, to exceed the bounds of reasonableness.[25] The Florida court's interpretation of "all terms" seems to contradict the understanding of what the voters of the state (which constituted 65% of the electorate) had in mind when they voted for that amendment. This interpretation is at odds with the words of the amendment that indicated that all terms would include "parole or probation." It would also cause confusion and wreak havoc by jeopardizing the voting eligibility of thousands and thousands of would-be voters, who would, thanks to the inadequacy of state records, have no way of knowing or even finding out whether their debts were paid or how much they owed. In the federal litigation that eventually ensued, the district court specifically found, on the basis of extensive testimony, that Florida's records indicating how much these would-be voters owed as fees, costs, fines, or even restitution to victims were incomplete and unreliable, and that it would take a good number of years for the state to ascertain how much they owed.

Even if the Florida legislature and court's construction of the phrase "all terms" is accepted as binding by the federal courts, the question remained whether that construction of the amendment to the Florida constitution is consistent with the federal Constitution. The difficulties of implementing the law as it was construed raise the most serious questions of due process, for the law puts a burden on would-be voters that, in all fairness, is extremely difficult if not impossible to discharge. In addition, the requirement to pay these amounts, or specifically fees and costs, to the state as a condition of voting appears to offend the Twenty-Fourth Amendment of the U.S. Constitution (which declares that the right to vote in federal elections shall not be denied for "failure to pay a poll tax or other tax"). It also appears to offend the Equal Protection Clause, which had, at least before *Richardson v. Ramirez* in 1974, been construed to require strict scrutiny of any state law that selectively distributes the franchise. Recall the decision in *Harper v. Virginia Board of Elections*, which concluded on this note: "Wealth or fee paying has, in our view, no relation to voting qualifications; the right to vote is too precious, too fundamental to be so burdened or conditioned."

Soon after the Florida Supreme Court approved of the legislature's interpretation of the phrase "all terms," the would-be voters commenced a suit in federal district court challenging this limitation of the right to vote that would be imposed as a result of this interpretation. In October 2019, the district court issued a preliminary injunction against the implementation of the Florida Supreme Court's interpretation of "all terms."[26] In so doing, the district judge applied the ordinary rules governing the issuance of interlocutory relief. He assessed the likelihood of the plaintiffs obtaining a permanent injunction after a full trial on the merits and the harm likely to be caused by the ban on voting from going immediately into effect (compared to the harm that might be caused by the issuance of the preliminary injunction). A panel of the Eleventh Circuit Court of Appeals affirmed the issuance of the preliminary injunction by the district judge.[27]

On May 24, 2020, after an eight-day trial, the district judge issued a permanent injunction prohibiting the contested interpretation from going into effect.[28] However, because the district judge conceived of the wrong in individualistic terms—not as an offense to democracy or a breach of its coextensionality requirement, but as an unfair burden on individuals seeking to vote—the remedy was limited. Rather than striking down this qualification for voting altogether, the district court allowed would-be voters to seek an advisory opinion from a state electoral agency about the amount owed and also allowed any would-be voter to opt out of paying the amount specified by the state agency by filing a statement indicating that they were unable to pay it. On July 1, 2020, the Eleventh Circuit, acting en banc, issued a stay of the district court's ruling pending its review of the merits. The Eleventh Circuit did not issue an opinion when it issued that stay of the permanent injunction.

Florida was scheduled to hold its primary for the 2020 election on July 20, only a few weeks after the circuit court issued a stay of the district court's permanent injunction. The plaintiffs were eager to vote in the coming primary and for that reason sought emergency relief in the United States Supreme Court. They wanted the Supreme Court to stay the Eleventh Circuit's stay, which would have the effect of allowing the district court's permanent injunction—in effect enabling ex-felons with outstanding fines and fees to vote—to go into effect while an appeal by the state was being prosecuted.

On July 16, the Supreme Court denied the application for a stay of the Eleventh Circuit's stay.[29] No opinion was issued to justify that action, but Justice Sotomayor understood the significance of the Court's action. She filed a dissent that Justices Ginsburg and Kagan joined. (The failure of Justice Breyer, who had on an earlier occasion written on *Our Democratic Constitution*,[30] was conspicuous.)

The summary action that the plaintiffs sought from the Supreme Court is truly exceptionable—the stay of a stay—and we must be careful not to read too much into the Court's refusal to accord the plaintiffs the relief they sought. Yet Sotomayor carefully explained how this case met the well-established standards for such extraordinary action. The Eleventh Circuit's stay would, Sotomayor said, prevent about 700,000 persons from participating in the primary—from exercising a right long-deemed precious or fundamental. The harm to the state that would be caused by the Supreme Court staying the Eleventh Circuit's stay paled in comparison. The action of the district court granting a permanent injunction against conditioning the right to vote on the payment of all fines, fees, costs, and victim restitution was well in accord with previous decisions of the Supreme Court, as the decision of the Eleventh Circuit panel made clear when it approved, in 2019, the preliminary injunction that the district court had issued.

On September 11, 2020—months after the July primary and roughly two months before the November 2020 general elections—the Eleventh Circuit issued its decision reversing the decision of the district court and vacating the permanent injunction it had issued.[31] The Eleventh Circuit accepted the Florida legislature's interpretation of the phrase "all terms" that was approved by the Florida Supreme Court and then went on to dismiss all the federal constitutional objections to that interpretation and the barrier it imposed on ex-felons trying to vote. The Eleventh Circuit was sharply divided, six to four. The majority took up each of the federal constitutional claims advanced against the imposition of financial obligations as a condition of voting, and in so doing it appeared to take *Richardson v. Ramirez* as a North Star, even though that decision had, after *Hunter v. Underwood*, been reduced to a political contrivance.

Under *Hunter v. Underwood*, a person—white or Black—disenfranchised because he or she was convicted of a crime might bring a claim under Section 1 of the Fourteenth Amendment. But the Eleventh Circuit read *Richardson v. Ramirez* to deny this would-be voter the benefit of the fundamental rights branch of strict scrutiny, even though Rehnquist had explicitly refused to rule on that issue. He only ruled that Section 2 of the Fourteenth Amendment precluded a consideration of that claim on its merits. The Eleventh Circuit also brushed aside the gross unfairness of a rule that denies ex-felons the right to vote because they have failed to discharge financial obligations that were for the most part unknown and unknowable. The Eleventh Circuit justified this particular ruling on the ground that those who vote cannot be criminally convicted for electoral fraud unless the prosecutor is able to show that the voter knew he or she was not eligible. Vote first and take your chances. The word "democracy" never appeared in the opinion of the Eleventh Circuit.[32]

Those representing the would-be voters in Florida did not apply for certiorari in the Supreme Court. It is always perilous to speculate on the reasons for such a decision, but fear of losing is certainly a plausible one. A loss on the merits in the Supreme Court would not only entail a waste of resources, but it might unfortunately establish a model to be used in other states for stymying efforts to restore the right to vote to ex-felons. Such a fear of affirmance could have been fueled by the unwillingness of the Supreme Court in July to stay the stay of the Eleventh Circuit. It might have also been fueled by the fact that, on September 18, 2020, a week after the Eleventh Circuit handed down its decision, Justice Ruth Bader Ginsburg, who had dissented from the earlier action of the Supreme Court, died. President Donald Trump was then in the White House, and he had the prerogative of filling that vacancy.

In this way, the Florida litigation revealed the larger significance of *Richardson v. Ramirez*: the Court renounced the power, at least when it came to laws disenfranchising ex-felons, to extend the franchise and honor the democratic principle of coextensionality—letting those who are ruled choose their rulers. Today, several million citizens, once convicted of a felony but who fully served their sentences, are denied the right to vote in eleven states.[33] In bemoaning this consequence of *Richardson v. Ramirez* and the regime it introduced, I do not mean to ignore the shortcomings of the legal doctrine—the fundamental rights branch of strict scrutiny—that was used by counsel and then Thurgood Marshall in dissent to attack state laws requiring the disenfranchisement of ex-felons. Treating denials of the right to vote as nothing more than a trigger of strict scrutiny disparages that right and misleads. It suggests that the disenfranchisement is a denial of equal protection when in fact the wrong inflicted by the state law disenfranchising ex-felons is of another character altogether—a failure of the state to honor the democratic character of the Constitution and the right to vote that it implies.

A judge that sees these shortcomings of the strict scrutiny test and is committed to protecting democracy from state laws disenfranchising ex-felons cannot stop by rejecting strict scrutiny. The judge must go on and announce doctrine that fully and adequately reflects the democratic aspirations of the Constitution and the principle of coextensionality. Traces, but only traces, of such an approach appear in Marshall's dissent in *Richardson v. Ramirez*. The formal framework he offered was equal protection, but all the work was done by democracy. In my view, however, the formal framework should accord with the substantive principle. Marshall's dissent should have been based on democracy not equal protection. Although such a fusion of form and substance might not have changed the outcome in *Richardson v. Ramirez*, let us not be naïve, it would have made the stakes clearer and, in that way, enhanced the jurisprudential significance of the dissent.

CITIZENSHIP AND THE REQUIREMENT
OF COEXTENSIONALITY

In pursuit of political freedom, the coextensionality principle—requiring all who are ruled to choose their rulers—calls for an ever-increasing extension of the franchise.

The Supreme Court turned its back on this principle in 1974 when it allowed the disenfranchisement of ex-felons, and this stance has recently been reinforced by the experience in Florida. With the approval of the Florida Supreme Court and legislature and then the Eleventh Circuit, the governor spearheaded a campaign to deny force to a state referendum that sought to honor the principle of coextensionality.

Yet, I emphasize, the coextensionality principle lives on, not just in the historic amendments that extended the franchise to Blacks and women, but also in the indelible experience of the 1960s. This was a period in the history of democracy that was defined by the voter registration drive of SNCC, the voting rights litigation program of the Department of Justice, the formation of the Mississippi Freedom Democratic Party, the march from Selma to Montgomery, the Voting Rights Act of 1965, and the landmark decisions of the Supreme Court in *Reynolds v. Sims* and *Harper v. Virginia Board of Elections*, both of which were founded on a recognition of the preciousness of the right to vote.

Even during the halcyon days for democracy of the 1960s, it was well understood that, as is true of any principle, there are limits on coextensionality. The principle of coextensionality does not require extending the franchise to those who have been convicted of a crime and are presently incarcerated or still subject to the terms of parole or probation. Nor does it require the enfranchisement of those involuntarily confined to mental hospitals. These people are wards of the state and thus confront the overwhelming power of the state in its authoritarian, rather than democratic, guise. Another and more contentious limitation on the democratic coextensionality principle involves people residing in the United States who are not citizens of the United States.

Some of those who fall into this category reside in the United States for short periods of time, others for decades. Some are here illegally because they entered the country surreptitiously, and others who are here illegally have overstayed their visas. Among those noncitizens here legally, some have chosen not to apply for citizenship for various reasons, some political, some entirely personal. Others have not yet had the opportunity to fulfil the requirements of applying for citizenship. In all these cases, people who are not citizens and thus have not affirmed their loyalty to the Constitution do not enjoy the right to vote that stems from the Constitution.[34] The denial of the right to vote to non-citizens would be all the more compelling if that right were viewed not as implicit or immanent in the Constitution as a whole, but rather, as some argue, based on the provision protecting the privileges and immunities of citizens of the United States.

Of course, recognition of the federal constitutional right to vote and its limits does not preclude state and local authorities from crafting their own right to vote and conferring it upon communities living within their borders. The constitutionality of such a practice, now existing in some localities, requires that this local right to vote extends to the elections of officials who only have local responsibilities. Like many of the enumerated rights of the Bill of Rights, the federal constitutional right to vote should be viewed as a floor, not as a ceiling.

For this reason, I do not view the practice of requiring American citizenship as a condition for voting as a betrayal of the democratic promise of the Constitution and the principle of coextensionality. Of another character altogether is the practice of denying American citizens the right to vote in federal elections simply because they live, not in one of the fifty states, but either in the District of Columbia (the seat of government) or, as in the case of Puerto Rico, a territory of the United States. Today Puerto Rico has a population of over 3 million, while the District of Columbia has a population of over 700,000. These populations are, in crucial respects, governed by Congress and the President. They are subject to federal law, yet the adult members of these communities are denied the right to participate fully in the process of choosing these federal officials simply because of where they happen to live. They are treated as subjects not as citizens, for they are denied the essential prerogative that belongs to citizens in a democratic society.

The District of Columbia is the seat of government envisioned by the Constitution. Puerto Rico was acquired by the United States as a result of the Spanish-American War of 1898, and ever since has been held as a territory of the United States. Today it is deemed a Commonwealth. In addition to Puerto Rico, the United States exercises dominion over four other territories, though they are more sparsely populated than Puerto Rico. Three of these territories are in the Pacific—Guam, the Northern Mariana Islands, and American Samoa—one—the Virgin Islands—is in the Caribbean.

Like Puerto Rico, Guam was captured by the United States forces in the Spanish-American War of 1898 and then ceded to the United States by Spain in the peace treaty. Guam was occupied by Japanese forces from 1941 to 1944, at which time it was recovered by the United States and held as a territory ever since. It currently has a population of about 170,000.

In 1899, the Northern Mariana Islands were sold by Spain to Germany. In 1914, soon after the outbreak of war in Europe, Japan took possession of these islands from Germany. In 1920 the League of Nations placed these islands under the mandate of Japan. In 1944 the United States captured these islands and first administered them under the auspices of the United Nations. Eventually these islands, like Puerto Rico, were given commonwealth status, subject to the dominion of the United States. The commonwealth of the Northern Mariana Islands has a population of about 58,000.

The third territory in the Pacific is American Samoa. It consists of a number of islands (Tutuila, Tau, Olosega, Ofu, and Aunuu) which have a total population of about 50,000. Under considerable pressure by the United States, which included financial inducements, these islands were ceded to the United States by the chiefs of local tribes at the very beginning of the twentieth century.

The fourth of these sparsely populated territories is the Virgin Islands, which largely consists of three large islands in the Caribbean—St. Croix, St. Thomas, and St. John—as well as fifty surrounding islands, all minor. The United States purchased the Virgin Islands in 1917 from Denmark at a price of $25 million, and they have been held by the United States ever since. The Virgin Islands have a population of about 106,000.

The Fourteenth Amendment provides that "All persons born or naturalized in the United States and subject to the jurisdiction thereof are citizens of the United States and of the state wherein they reside." Arguably, all the persons born in these four territories, Puerto Rico, and the District of Columbia are subject to the jurisdiction of the United States and thus might be deemed, under the terms of the Fourteenth Amendment, American citizens. On the other hand, in addition to United States citizenship, the portion of the Fourteenth Amendment conferring state citizenship to these individuals wherever they reside might imply that the rule conferring United States citizenship to those born in the United States and subject to its jurisdiction might only apply to persons born in one of the states or in a territory that has become a state.

No one doubts that persons born in the District of Columbia are citizens of the United States. After all, it is the seat of government. In some cases, the persons born in the territories, most assuredly those born in Puerto Rico, can claim, by virtue of congressional statutes, United States citizenship.[35] As citizens, persons born in Puerto Rico have the right to move to one of the fifty states. If they do, and satisfy the state's other requirements for voting (for example, age and residence), they can participate in the elections for President and Vice President, for members of the House of Representatives representing the district in which they live, and for the senators who represent the state in which they reside. They have no such right if they remain in Puerto Rico. The same is true for residents of the District of Columbia because they are United States citizens. They may vote for federal officers if they move to one of the states, say, Maryland or Virginia. If these individuals remain in the District of Columbia, however, their right to participate in the elections of federal officials is limited or denied, even if these individuals satisfy the other requirements for voting.

The District of Columbia and the four territories have local governing institutions. Residents are able to participate fully in the election of those who staff the local executive and legislative branches. The problem arises, however, because those living in the District of Columbia or the territories are also subject to the statutes enacted by Congress (unless some special provision makes them locally inapplicable). They are also subject to the action of the President implementing those statutes or otherwise exercising his powers under Article II of the Constitution. Although the residents of the

District of Columbia can, by virtue of a congressional enactment, vote for the President and Vice President (the District is allocated a number of electors as though it were a state, "but in no event more than the least populous State"), the residents of the territories do not enjoy this limited prerogative. Moreover, the residents of the District of Columbia and the four territories have no representation whatsoever in the Senate. They can elect someone who voice their views or represent their interests in the House of Representatives, but that person can only act as a spokesperson and does not have a vote.

The breaches of the requirement of coextensionality effectuated by these electoral arrangements are manifest. Officers of the federal government have authority to rule over the District of Columbia and the four territories and yet these officers are not selected, in any meaningful sense, by those who are subject to their authority. It should be acknowledged that the reason for this disenfranchisement may be weightier than those that we encountered to justify the other rules that disenfranchise American citizens, such as those applicable to ex-felons. The disenfranchisement of American citizens who are residents of the District of Columbia or the four territories may be attributable to the anomalous status of these particular entities within the structure of the Constitution, which treats the states as the constituent units of the Union. States are the units for allocating representation in the Senate and in the House; and the Electoral College extends their importance into the election of the President and Vice President.

Accordingly, the disenfranchisement of those American citizens residing in the District of Columbia and the territories might be said to be attributable, not, as is the case of ex-felons, to the excessively harsh, moralistic, and perhaps outdated views about those who have been convicted of committing a crime, but rather to the design of the Constitution that makes prominent use of the states. As a result, the role of the judiciary in extending the franchise to the residents of the

District of Columbia and the territories may be more limited, certainly unlikely. Other means of reform may, however, be available.

The status of the District of Columbia and the territories might be changed to fit into the design of the Constitution. The District of Columbia and Puerto Rico might become states or, in the case of all the territories including Puerto Rico, the dominion of the United States might be renounced. Even if such reforms are not politically feasible or, as seems true for the sparsely populated territories, not prudent, the feature of the Constitution responsible for this disenfranchisement might be revised. The role of the states in the structure of the Constitution dates from its original formulation in the summer of 1787. That design was not intended to last for eternity—it could be changed, certainly by an amendment that makes special arrangements for the District of Columbia and enumerated territories. Such an amendment would become especially appealing once we understand that the original design interferes with the realization of yet another and arguably more overarching feature of the Constitution—its democratic promise. Denying citizens of the United States the right to vote is abhorrent to the democratic aspirations of the Constitution as it stands today and to the coextensionality principle to which it gives rise—allowing those who are ruled to choose their rulers.

CHAPTER 3

. . .

The Duty of Facilitation

IN THE PREVIOUS chapter, we dealt with the power of the states to determine who is entitled to vote. Because the political freedom that democracy promises arises only when those who are ruled are able to select their rulers, democracy itself, as a theory of government, requires extending the franchise to all who are ruled—the requirement of coextensionality. In this chapter, I deal not with state rules that selectively distribute the franchise or establish the qualifications for voting. Rather, the focus is on the rules enacted by the states for managing the electoral process—those that determine the time, place, and manner of voting.

This shift of focus must be acknowledged, though even in this domain, vigilance is required. We must be mindful of the essential purpose of democracy—to enable the ruled to choose their rulers— carefully scrutinize these managerial exercises of state power, and honor a requirement analogous to coextensionality. I call it the duty of facilitation. States must do all that they can be reasonably expected to do in enhancing and facilitating the participation in the electoral process of all those who are qualified to vote. Like coextensionality,

Why We Vote. Owen Fiss, Oxford University Press. © Owen Fiss 2024.
DOI: 10.1093/oso/9780197746387.003.0004

the duty of facilitation seeks to enhance the freedom generated by democracy and stems from our attachment to that goal.

The Constitution entrusts the states, at least as an initial matter, with the power to administer and thus manage elections, whether the election be for federal or state officers.[1] States must decide, for example, how and when people are to be registered to vote, whether the votes will be cast in person or through the mail or online, and whether the election will be held on a single day or if people will be allowed to cast their votes over a sustained period of time. The states must also decide how individuals wishing to vote shall establish their qualifications to vote and how officials shall make certain that each person has only voted once. Because the electoral process is the source of the freedom that democracy generates, it is also, I argue, incumbent on the states to discharge their managerial responsibilities in a way that facilitates participation in the electoral process. The greater the participation of those who are ruled and who are qualified to vote, the greater the freedom. Accordingly, states should do their best to make certain that those who are ruled and qualified to vote are able, as a purely practical matter, to select their rulers.

State administration of elections has often been scrutinized through the lens of constitutional provisions aimed at guaranteeing equality because the administrative rules enacted by the state may well have an unequal impact on various subgroups among qualified voters. For example, restricting the number of places where people must go to vote or locating polling stations some distance from heavily populated neighborhoods is likely to have an adverse impact on the ability to vote of the poor, disabled, and aged. This impact might even have a racial dimension. Most of the poor are white, but a disproportionate number of Blacks are poor. Even today, long after the beginning of the Second Reconstruction in 1954 and the emergence of a Black middle class, Blacks are nearly twice as likely as whites to live in poverty. The higher incidence of poverty among Blacks constitutes a vestige of three different, interlocking dynamics: a slave system that was defined wholly in racial terms, the enactment of Jim Crow laws that had, for almost a century, restricted educational and employment opportunities for Blacks, and the concentration of Blacks in the agricultural economy of the South at the conclusion of the Civil War.

The disparate impacts of the rules governing elections, especially the racial one, may give rise to a claim of redress under federal or state laws requiring equality. Exclusions from the franchise, even if due not to intentional targeting but the interaction between state laws and social circumstance, has the consequence of perpetuating or even magnifying the disadvantages of being poor. Exclusion is still an exclusion even if it is partly due to social circumstances. It will leave its mark on those who are in fact excluded and impair their capacity to advocate for policies and programs especially responsive to their needs.

I am thoroughly sympathetic to such egalitarian claims and acknowledge the very special force of these claims when advanced by Blacks under the Fourteenth and Fifteenth Amendments and the Voting Rights Act of 1965. Yet what needs to be stressed here is that democracy itself, as a guiding ideal of the Constitution, gives rise to yet another claim for redress, one that arises from liberty rather than equality. Democracy is valued because it generates political freedom, and its capacity to do so depends, as I said, on the premise that those who are ruled are able to choose their rulers. This requires the state to minimize the practical barriers or impediments that would-be voters are likely to encounter in their attempt to vote.

Breaches of this duty are not only of concern to minorities. Recent history has shown that sometimes circumstances arise that make it difficult, as a purely practical matter, for large swaths of the population to exercise the right to vote. The recent experience with the COVID-19 pandemic during the 2020 presidential election reveals as much. We vote in secret, but on Election Day polling places are the loci where would-be voters congregate and are likely to come into contact with their neighbors as well as with polling officials. In the middle of a pandemic, such person-to-person contacts may be especially dangerous. In such circumstances, the states should be required, as the duty of facilitation dictates, to liberalize the rules for utilizing absentee ballots or, in order to avoid congestion at polling sites, to extend the period for voting—for example, by turning the election day into an election week.

Almost every managerial decision, even one determining the number and location of polling sites, will have significant financial consequences for the community. Although the duty of facilitation does not require the state to ignore these consequences, every community can be expected to commit the financial resources necessary to make voting reasonably available to all its members. The legitimacy of the outcome of an election depends on the degree to which all those who are qualified to vote have in fact voted. The discharge of that duty does not compel financial disaster nor the neglect of the other needs of the community. It only requires that the expenditures needed for running an election be given a special priority and that the use of taxing and spending power reflect that priority. Voting allows people to participate in the process through which they choose their rulers and, in so doing, it generates the freedom that democracy confers on the people as a whole.

In 1993, Congress gave concrete expression to the duty of facilitation by enacting the National Voter Registration Act. This law seeks to further the democratic ideal by requiring states to provide would-be voters with the opportunity to register to vote at the time they applied for a driver's license or sought to renew their license. Similarly, the statute requires that voter registration opportunities be available at all offices that provide public assistance or special services to persons with disabilities. The statute also provides a standard federal registration form that must be used by the states.

As a purely technical matter, Congress limited the reach of this statute to the election of federal officials. The practical import of this limitation is not at all clear, since the states typically require would-be voters to register only once, and that registration would cover elections of both state and federal officials. Moreover, in enacting this statute, Congress acted on broader democratic principles aimed at enlarging the domain of political freedom—principles that make no distinction between elections for choosing state or federal officials. The Senate report declared that "the purpose of our election process is not to test the fortitude and determination of the voter, but to discern the will of the majority." The statute itself affirms that "the right of citizens of the United States to vote is a fundamental right" and that it "is a duty of the federal, state, and local governments to promote the exercise of that right."

In justifying the 1993 Act in these terms, Congress drew on the conception of voting—the right to vote is a fundamental right—that was propounded by the Supreme Court in such landmark decisions as *Reynolds v. Sims* and *Harper v. Virginia Board of Elections*. In 1993, Congress used the principle announced in those cases to insist upon and give content to the duty of facilitation in the registration process. However, the impulse that accounted for the 1993 Act soon vanished, at least in the political domain. In November 1994, Republicans gained control of the House of Representatives and chose Newt Gingrich as Speaker of the House. By 1996, under Gingrich's leadership, Congress had enacted a number of measures that sought to curb many of the progressive policies and programs that had, as recently as the early 1990s, once flourished. Statutes were enacted restricting prison reform litigation, limiting welfare assistance to a total of five years for Americans, denying any such assistance, including food stamps, to aliens, whether they were in the United States legally or not, and curtailing the availability of habeas corpus.

During Gingrich's tenure, there was no impulse whatsoever in Congress to protect, much less facilitate, the exercise of voting rights, even though such protective measures might have been inspired and shaped by the Constitution. This attitude continued long after Gingrich left Congress, indeed even after the Democrats had regained control of the House, for even then, Republicans largely remained in control of the Senate. Congress's stance toward voting rights accounts for the failure of the legislature to respond to the 2013 decision of the Supreme Court in *Shelby County v. Holder*, which, as explained in Chapter 2, rendered the preclearance procedures of the Voting Rights Act of 1965 inoperative. In that case, the Court declared the coverage formula needed to activate the preclearance anachronistic and thus invalid. In the wake of *Shelby County*, many proposals for updating and correcting the coverage formula were devised and introduced on the floor of Congress, but none were enacted to vindicate democratic principles.

In this environment, Congress could not be reasonably expected to effectively supervise the managerial decisions of the states governing elections. As a result, the burden fell on the Supreme Court to do so. While the default of Congress explains the need for the judiciary to act, it does not constitute the justification for that action, which arises from a recognition of democracy as a guiding ideal of the Constitution and the importance attached to the right to vote in the democratic system of government. The prerogative, indeed the duty of the Court to review the managerial role of the states governing elections, is based on the belief, to borrow language used by the sponsors of the 1993 Act, that the purpose of the electoral process is not to test the fortitude and determination of the voters, but to discern the will of the majority.

The sponsors of the 1993 Act drew on the language of *Reynolds v. Sims* and *Harper v. Virginia Board of Elections*, proclaiming the preciousness or fundamentality of the right to vote. This characterization of the right to vote occurred in cases that turned on the application of the Equal Protection Clause. In these cases, interferences with the right to vote were treated as a trigger of strict scrutiny requiring the state to justify the contested measure as necessary for the pursuit of some compelling public interest. In Chapter 1, and again in Chapter 2, I pointed to the shortcomings of such an approach to voting rights: it disparages the right to vote and the premise of the test misleads. It assumes that the constitutional wrong condemned in those cases constituted an affront to equal protection rather than, as I insisted, a betrayal of the democratic character of the Constitution. I then maintained that the right to vote should be seen not simply as a trigger of strict scrutiny, but as an independent, substantive constitutional right of its own, much like the enumerated rights set forth in the Bill of Rights.

A law selectively distributing the franchise, such as the one that denies ex-felons the right to vote, should be seen as a breach of that right. That was the thrust of Chapter 2. In this chapter, I maintain that a law regulating the management of an election might also be deemed a breach of the right to vote, for it limits or curtails the exercise of that right, and, further, that the burden falls on the judiciary to determine the legitimacy of the limits imposed by the state on the exercise of that right. In this regard, established doctrine governing the right of free speech might be instructive.

A law prohibiting criticism of public officials would surely violate the First Amendment guarantee of freedom of speech. So might a law that, without regard to content, burdens those planning a parade on the public streets to protest a public policy by requiring them to post a bond or pay for the additional police needed to divert traffic. Those organizing the protest might well argue that such requirements limit the exercise of the right to speak freely. In passing on that claim, the court must assess the dangers to the exercise of the right to speak and the justification that might be mustered to defend those limits. Similarly, I would maintain that a law limiting the exercise of the right to vote, without regard to how that vote might be cast, must be judicially assessed. The court must determine, not whether the law constitutes a denial of equal protection, but whether the law accords with the democratic ideal of the Constitution and the right to which that ideal gives rise—the right to vote. The duty of facilitation, seen as an instrument for enhancing the political freedom that democracy generates, is rooted in this understanding of the right to vote, as an independent, substantive constitutional right and the basis for judging laws that limit the exercise of the right.

A good number but not all of the managerial decisions of the states that were enacted in recent years have been predicated, at least in name, on the desire to prevent electoral fraud and preserve the integrity of the electoral process. Only qualified voters should be allowed to vote, and they should only vote once. These are indeed commendable aspirations and might well be applauded, yet one could readily see the dangers that lurked within them. If the procedures are too stringent, for example, by requiring extravagant and highly burdensome proof of eligibility, some who are entitled to vote will turn their back on voting or be effectively barred from the process because they do not have the funds or time to secure the necessary documentation. On the other hand, if these procedures are too lax, people who are not in fact entitled to vote will vote and in that way dilute the votes of those who are entitled to vote. In these cases, it is fair to say that a freedom appears on both sides of the ledger—it is both enhanced and constrained by the state regulation—and as a result the duty of facilitation must be adjusted to account for this duality.

THE COURT SPEAKS, THOUGH IN A MULTITUDE OF TONGUES

The complexity and difficulty of resolving the conflict entailed in the exercise of the managerial power of the states over elections is revealed in the Supreme Court's 2008 decision in *Crawford v. Marion County Election Board*.[2] It stemmed from an Indiana decision to tighten the procedure for making certain that the person who presents him or herself to the voting official on Election Day is the person who had previously registered to vote. The Indiana statute required every person who wishes to vote to possess a photo ID that was issued by a government agency. The measure honored passports, since they were issued by the Department of State of the United States, but the new law primarily contemplated that the required photo ID would be issued by the Indiana Bureau of Motor Vehicles (BMV), which regularly provides photo IDs when it issues driving licenses.

Although the practical burden of obtaining such a photo ID is not insurmountable, it is far more than a mere inconvenience, compared to the means citizens customarily use to identify themselves at the polls, such as library cards, utility bills, credit cards, or IDs issued by their employer. Securing the government-issued photo ID, such as a passport, may entail paying fees to the issuing agency or assembling documents that are extremely hard to find. Securing a photo ID from the BMV may also require extended trips on public transportation to reach the offices of the agency issuing the photo ID, even if it be the BMV, since the BMV offices tend to be more sparsely located than polling places. A visit to a local BMV office might even require the applicant to take off time from work, given the time required to reach a BMV office and the time required to obtain service at this office. One could thus readily understand how the need to obtain a government-issued photo ID might well have the practical effect of preventing many members of the electorate from voting, particularly the physically disabled, the aged, the poor, and those living in scattered and distant rural areas.

By the time the Court confronted this issue, almost forty years had passed since the presidential election of 1968 and the turnover in personnel on the Court that primarily accounted for its 1974 decision in *Richardson v. Ramirez* (the principal subject of the previous chapter). During this period the nation experienced yet another cycle of personnel changes on the High Court. Indeed, all of the persons President Nixon had appointed in the first cycle had, by 2008, stepped down, as had the spark plugs of the Warren Court— William Douglas, William Brennan, and Thurgood Marshall—who had participated in *Richardson v. Ramirez*, though they dissented.

The vacancies occurring between *Ramirez* and *Crawford* were filled by a politically diverse array of presidents. Bill Clinton (1992– 2000), a Democrat, appointed two justices—Stephen Breyer and Ruth Bader Ginsburg, both of whom sat on the Court that decided *Crawford*. All the other justices on the *Crawford* case—John Paul Stevens, Antonin Scalia, Anthony Kennedy, David Souter, Clarence Thomas, Samuel Alito, and John Roberts—were appointed by Republican presidents: either Gerald Ford (197–1977), Ronald Reagan (1981–1989), George H.W. Bush (1989–1993), or George W. Bush (2001–2009). There were important differences among these presidents and their appointees but, speaking generally, the ideological profile of a controlling majority in 2008 was the same as the majority that decided *Richardson v. Ramirez* in 1974. For the most part, they looked askance and, in some instances, were downright antagonistic to the landmark decisions of the Warren Court that had given content to the democratic ideal of the Constitution, stressed the importance of the right to vote, and inspired the 1993 National Voter Registration Act.

Unsurprisingly, *Crawford* became a highly visible conflict over the power of the states to manage elections. The Court was flooded with a plethora of amicus briefs submitted by a wide variety of civic and political organizations. Moreover, given the ideological profile of the justices and the presidents who appointed them, it was no surprise that the case divided the Court. The extent of the division, however, was startling, almost dizzying. Although a majority of the justices voted to sustain the Indiana photo ID requirement and thus put the duty of facilitation in doubt, the nine justices were arrayed in four different camps, each camp issuing its own opinion, and as a consequence, no opinion commanded a majority, nor even a plurality.

Three justices dissented—David Souter, Ruth Bader Ginsburg, and Stephen Breyer. Even the dissenters were divided. Souter wrote an opinion that Ginsburg joined. Breyer also wrote a dissenting opinion. It set forth a doctrinal framework or test that differed from Souter's. No other justice joined Breyer's opinion. The six justices who voted to uphold the Indiana law were also divided. One group consisted of Stevens, Roberts, and Kennedy. They joined an opinion written by Stevens, who purportedly used the same doctrinal framework as Souter but came to the opposite conclusion. Justice Scalia filed yet another opinion sustaining the Indiana law, and that opinion was joined by Thomas and Alito. Scalia's opinion largely rejected the doctrinal framework employed by both Stevens and Souter in their opinions, as well as the one used by Breyer. Justice Scalia professed indifference, as a constitutional matter, to the practical barriers to exercising the right to vote that were created by the Indiana law and, in essence, even refused to inquire into the impact of the Indiana law on voters.

SOUTER VS. STEVENS AND THE DIFFERING APPLICATIONS
OF THE SAME TEST

Both Stevens and Souter applied the same doctrinal test, a sliding scale balancing test, to judge the Indiana statute. This test was first formulated by Stevens in a 1983 case—*Anderson v. Celebrezze*— in which an independent candidate for the presidency—John Anderson—sought access to the Ohio ballot.[3] Stevens had used the test in that case to determine whether the Ohio law requiring early filing by independents abridged the right to free political association, a right that the Court itself had inferred from the First Amendment guarantee of free speech. Stevens specifically disavowed any reliance on equal protection, which had been used in 1968 as the basis of setting aside another law of Ohio that fenced out independents and which became the fountainhead of the law governing ballot access. In *Crawford*, the sliding scale balancing test was used by Stevens as a substitute for strict scrutiny, which governed the application of equal protection rather than associational freedom.

Souter was not on the Court at the time of *Anderson v. Celebrezze*, but he had, in 1992, joined a majority opinion in *Burdick v. Takushi*, which upheld Hawaii's ban on write-in candidates.[4] The majority opinion in that case was written by Justice White, who used the sliding scale balancing test, though he paid no special attention to whether the underlying constitutional right was equal protection or associational freedom.[5] Similarly, Souter in *Crawford* was remarkably inattentive to the underlying right used to challenge the Indiana law. This unexplained or even unacknowledged migration of the sliding scale balancing test from associational freedom to equal protection and the relative indifference to the particular clause of the Constitution being implemented might reveal a deeper and more surprising truth: a good number of justices are prepared to recognize the constitutional status of the right to vote, although they dare not openly acknowledge that they do.

In adopting the sliding scale balancing test, both Stevens and Souter explicitly rejected the strict scrutiny test that was the hallmark of the Warren Court's jurisprudence on voting, as manifest in cases such as *Kramer v. Union Free School District No. 15*. They claimed that strict scrutiny did not permit a consideration of the legitimate interest a state might have for restricting the right to vote. Borrowing language from his *Anderson* opinion, Stevens spoke disparagingly of strict scrutiny as a " 'litmus test' that would neatly separate valid from invalid restrictions" without regard to the interest that the state might put forward to justify a restriction.[6] Similarly, Souter defended his rejection of strict scrutiny on the ground that it did not take into account "the legitimacy of interests on both sides."[7]

To me these complaints about strict scrutiny seem unfounded. Strict scrutiny specifically allowed for a consideration of the interests a state might put forward to justify its regulation. It only required that these interests have a special importance or weightiness when it comes to justifying denials to the right to vote. On the other hand, I would say that strict scrutiny appears uniquely inappropriate in *Crawford* because the interference with the right to vote arises not from the selective distribution of the franchise, as it did in cases such as *Kramer*, but rather from the rules the state has enacted in administering the election and the barriers those rules have created for those wishing to exercise their right to vote. In other words, the state law in *Crawford* was being challenged on the basis of its effect, not on the basis of the criterion used by the state to distribute the franchise (sometimes referred to as intention or purpose). In such cases, there are necessarily going to be gradations of effect, and both Souter and Stevens properly wanted to have the burden of justification vary with the magnitude of the burden upon those wishing to vote—the essence of a sliding scale balancing test.

In contrast to strict scrutiny, both Stevens and Souter sought a test that was predicated on the interactive dynamic between the harm inflicted by the state law and the burden of justification. As Souter put it, he did not want a test that was "preset."[8] The greater the harm, the greater the burden of justification. Under the sliding scale balancing test, the state only needs to produce a compelling justification if the harm is "severe." If, however, the harm is "serious" as opposed to "severe," the state is put to the burden of producing a significant justification, and if the harm is "modest," then the state only need show that the law serves a legitimate or permissible purpose. Crucially, Souter's analysis of the Indiana law turned on his belief that the impact of the Indiana law was "serious," which would be measured in terms of the number of people who would, as a practical matter, be barred from voting. In contrast, Stevens insisted that since the Indiana law adversely affected only "a small number of voters,"[9] the preclusive impact was only "modest."

Focusing on this particular disagreement between Stevens and Souter reveals the quantitative dimension of the sliding scale balancing test: application of the test will in part turn on the number of people barred from voting, not simply whether some individual has, given his or her personal circumstances, been barred from voting. Such a quantitative understanding may seem in conflict with the purely individualistic character of the protection offered by some enumerated rights, for example, the right to the assistance of counsel in criminal proceedings, which tends to be an absolute protection for the individual: The infringement of that right does not depend on the number of persons who would be barred by a state law from consulting with, or receiving the assistance of, counsel. On the other hand, a systemic right such as the right to vote necessarily has a collective dimension. The right to vote is exercised by individuals, but the freedom that it secures belongs to the people as a people. Democracy, both as a constitutional ideal and a constitutional mandate, protects the rights of the ruled to choose their rulers and the freedom it generates is a political freedom. As a result, it is necessarily concerned with the proportion of people (the ruled) who would be excluded from participating in the election because, due to practical circumstances, they cannot meet the requirements set by the state for qualified voters to participate in the election (for example, possession of a government-issued photo ID).

Determining the number of people prevented from voting due to the photo ID requirement of Indiana is no easy task. Mathematical precision is not required, but some rough estimate is necessary in order to apply the sliding scale balancing test, for it depends on whether the burden created by the Indiana law is "modest," "serious," or "severe." The district court was prepared to assume that 43,000 would-be voters lacked the government-issued photo ID required by Indiana. The lawyers representing the state did not take issue with that estimate and were prepared to defend the law even if it could be assumed to have such a preclusive effect.

Souter began his analysis of the harm by acknowledging this concession. He also noted that the figure of 43,000 used by the district court represented about 1% of the voting age population of Indiana, and that was significantly less than the 6–10% figure estimated by a recently convened national commission on elections. Relying on the estimate of the national commission, Souter calculated that the Indiana photo ID requirement would prevent a much larger number of people from voting—250,000–400,000.

In addition, Souter considered a wide number of factors that might either increase or decrease the figure used by the district court, such as the location of BMV offices and the availability of public transportation to those offices. In each instance, Souter pointed to the special burden that obtaining the government issued photo ID would impose on the economically disadvantaged, the disabled, and the aged,[10] a group he described as "the poor and the weak,"[11] not to turn the underlying claim into one of equality, but only to have a more realistic appraisal of the consequences of the state requirement on democracy. By way of summarizing his analysis of the harm of the photo ID requirement, Souter concluded that the Indiana law would have the effect of barring "tens of thousands"[12] of would-be voters because of the difficulty they might have in obtaining the requisite photo ID. He fully appreciated that certain social circumstances, not just the decision of the state, were in part responsible for this preclusive impact, but, as he recognized and Stevens did not, disenfranchisement is disenfranchisement.[13]

Once Souter concluded that the Indiana photo ID law posed a "serious" (though not a "severe") burden on the ability of would-be voters, the sliding scale balancing test then required a judgment of whether the burden was justified by a public purpose. Unlike strict scrutiny, the public purpose required by the sliding scale test need not, in this instance, be "compelling," yet it must satisfy some intermediate standard, that is, it must be "important" or "substantial," not simply "reasonable" or "legitimate." Those who defended the law maintained that it was needed to preserve the "integrity of elections," understood in some abstract or general way, almost as though it were a sacred duty. Souter refused to accept such an approach. He insisted that the justification must be tightly tied to the measure being judged. What is the particular evil, Souter asked, that the photo ID requirement was designed to prevent, and how serious was that threat to the integrity of the election?

Souter acknowledged that the Indiana photo ID requirement would prevent impersonation at the time of voting. He did not deny the legitimacy of preventing this type of fraud, though he noted the absence of any evidence suggesting that this type of fraud was a common occurrence. Souter also explained why this type of fraud was rare and, even more, why it was unlikely to occur on a wholesale basis. These conjectures did not lead Souter to deny the legitimacy of the public purpose served by the measure, he only doubted its importance and significance, which under the sliding scale balancing test is to be weighed against its serious adverse effect—according to Souter, the disenfranchisement of, at the very least, "tens of thousands" of qualified voters.

Souter also acknowledged that, in considering whether the adverse effect was justified, some consideration must be given, first, to whether there are alternative ways by which that purpose—the prevention of impersonation—can be achieved and, second, whether these alternatives might be less burdensome on the right to vote than the state rule mandating the possession of a government-issued photo ID a condition of voting. In this context, Souter pointed to state laws criminalizing electoral fraud and concluded that relying on those laws and their deterrent effect to prevent impersonation was a less burdensome alternative than the photo ID requirement. They discouraged fraud, and at the same time do not prevent from voting those who were qualified to vote but found it very difficult if not impossible to make a trip to the BMV to obtain a photo ID or pay the fees necessary to obtain a US passport.

Stevens, in contrast, wrote his opinion in reverse. Under the sliding scale balancing test, the burden of justification varies with the magnitude of the wrong. It was thus odd that Justice Stevens began his opinion with an analysis of the justification of the photo ID requirement—to prevent fraud—and only turned to estimating the likely scope of the disenfranchisement in the concluding portion of his opinion. Once he reached this point, Stevens insisted, as I already noted, that the photo ID requirement would only burden "a small number of voters." At the very end of his opinion, Stevens added a footnote, surely written after Souter circulated his dissent, in which Stevens directly confronted and then specifically rejected Souter's estimate of the measure's impact on "tens of thousands."

In that footnote, Stevens first said that the district judge's estimate of 43,000 might be dated. The estimate was made at the time the Indiana statute was passed (2005) and, according to Stevens, it "tells us nothing about the number of the free photo identification cards issued since then."[14] In making this comment, Stevens was, in effect, faulting Souter for ignoring the developments that might have occurred in the period between, on the one hand, the enactment of a law and the near contemporaneous decision of the district court and, on the other hand, the issuance of the Supreme Court decision. However, to make much of these developments would unfortunately turn the Indiana law into a moving target with which no litigator could contend. Souter was, to be sure, less sanguine about the changes between 2005 and 2008, citing a recent newspaper article that described a lawsuit launched in 2008 trying to prevent the state from revoking up to 56,000 driver's licenses that did not match information contained in a Social Security database.

As a second ground of objection to Souter's figure of "tens of thousands," Stevens made a point in that very same footnote which seems, on reflection, more appropriate for a college debater than for a justice of the Supreme Court. He accused Souter of failing to take account of "how often elderly and indigent citizens have an opportunity to obtain a photo identification at a BMV, either during a routine outing with family or friends or during a special visit to the BMV arranged by a civic or political group such as the League of Women Voters or a political party."[15]

In reading Souter's opinion, one must inevitably be impressed by the precision and care of his analysis—of both the likely harm of the Indiana statute and the justification for the photo ID requirement. His method of applying the sliding scale balancing test stands in marked contrast to that of Stevens. This difference between the two—in the quality of the analysis and thus the result that it produced (one invalidating the Indiana statute, the other upholding it)—might be due to differences in the temperament or habits of mind of the two justices. More plausibly, however, it might be due to the different perspectives they each took on the importance of the right to vote.

Although Souter rejected strict scrutiny—which was to be triggered by interferences with a fundamental right—he began his opinion with a bold and striking acknowledgement of the fundamentality and preciousness of the right to vote. In fact, in *Crawford*, Souter quoted with approval Warren's assessment in *Reynolds v. Sims* about the preciousness of the right to vote and, I venture to say, was guided by this perspective in applying the sliding scale balancing test.[16]

Stevens, on the other hand, was unwilling to embrace the *Reynolds v. Sims* postulate about the preciousness and fundamentality of the right to vote. Although Stevens did not refer to *Reynolds v. Sims*, admittedly he cited one of *Reynold*'s progeny, *Harper v. Virginia Board of Elections*. Yet he did not acknowledge the role that the democratic postulate of *Reynolds v. Sims*—declaring the preciousness of the right to vote—had played in the majority's reasoning in *Harper*. In addition, Stevens obscured the significance of *Harper*'s holding by presenting it as a vindication of equality rather than the liberty generated by democracy. For him, the poll tax was invalidated in *Harper* simply because it "invidiously discriminate[s]."[17] While Souter reasoned from the freedom that democracy generates, Stevens reasoned from equality, and did a less than admirable job there.

In *Crawford*, both Stevens and Souter applied the same sliding scale balancing test, but only Souter's application of that test—guided by the importance he attached to the right to vote—gave some effect to the duty of facilitation. Like Souter, Breyer also dissented, but he offered an alternative—the so-called proportionality test—to the sliding scale balancing test.[18] Yet, compared to Souter's approach, proportionality did not further in any significant way the imposition of a duty on the states to facilitate the exercise of the right to vote.

The proportionality test requires a court to set aside a law when the harm it produces is vastly greater than the benefit it produces. More significantly for the case at hand, it requires a court to set aside a state law when the benefit the law produces can be achieved by less restrictive or burdensome alternatives. With this feature of the proportionality test in mind, Breyer maintained that the Indiana photo ID law was unnecessarily restrictive and that there were plenty of less onerous alternatives for achieving the purpose of the Indiana law. To support that conclusion, Breyer detailed the photo ID requirements of Florida and Georgia, both of which also sought to prevent impersonation, but did so in a way that was likely to have a less adverse impact than the Indiana requirement.

In this way, Breyer's dissent amplified Souter's consideration of alternatives to the Indiana photo-ID requirement. When Stevens originally formulated the test in the 1983 case involving access to the ballot for an independent candidate, he required that attention be paid to alternatives. In *Crawford*, however, Stevens did not pay much attention to the alternative strategies that Indiana might use to protect against fraud by impersonating a registered voter. In contrast to Stevens, in *Crawford* Souter stressed this feature of the sliding scale balancing test. He understood that an inquiry into whether the adverse impact of the measure was justified necessarily required a consideration of alternatives. Souter thus asked whether the purpose of the Indiana law—minimizing the risk of impersonation—could be achieved without denying "tens of thousands" their right to vote. In asking this question, Souter narrowed the gap between Breyer's proportionality test and his own sliding scale balancing test, and even more significantly, he narrowed the gap between the sliding scale balancing test and strict scrutiny. Under strict scrutiny, the consideration of alternatives explicitly occurs under the narrow tailoring requirement of that test.

SCALIA AND HIS STUDIED INDIFFERENCE TO THE EFFECTS OF THE STATE LAW MANAGING ELECTIONS

Justice Scalia introduced an entirely different perspective on the conflict of values presented by the Indiana voter ID requirement. In essence, he rejected any consideration of the impact of the state law on the exercise of the right to vote and thus repudiated the duty of facilitation in its entirety. Like Stevens and the two other justices who joined his opinion—Roberts and Kennedy—Scalia voted to uphold the Indiana law. However, Scalia's opinion, joined by Clarence Thomas and Samuel Alito, fully rejected the sliding scale balancing test used not just by Souter, but also by Stevens. I assume that he felt the same about Breyer's proportionality test, though he did not target it with any specificity.

Scalia's hostility to a sliding scale balancing test, or for that matter a proportionality test, stemmed from the fact that both these tests crucially depended on an assessment of the effect or impact attributable to the state law in question. For Scalia, such an inquiry is anathema to proper constitutional analysis. Citing the 1976 decision in *Washington v. Davis*, Scalia declared in his opinion in *Crawford* that the "Fourteenth Amendment does not regard neutral laws as invidious ones, *even when their burdens purportedly fall disproportionately on a protected class*."[19] The transgression of the rule of *Washington v. Davis* occasioned by the sliding scale balancing test was particularly egregious, Scalia added, because "the classes complaining of disparate impact are not even protected."[20] He then cited the key Supreme Court precedent denying that the poor, the disabled, or the aged are "protected classes" or, to put the point differently, denied them status as "suspect classes" and thus did not entitle them to heightened scrutiny of any law that has an adverse impact on them.

In pursuing this line of analysis, Scalia obscured the fact that the sliding scale balancing test used in *Crawford* was used to assess a claim designed to protect democracy and the freedom it generates, not equality or equal protection. Of course, Scalia's hostility to inquiries about the adverse effect of a state law was global in character, and thus invoking democracy as the basis of the claim of right was not likely to make a difference. Adding to his string of citations denying equal protection claims of a variety of groups (the poor, disabled, and aged), Scalia referred to his opinion for the Court in *Employment Division, Department of Human Resources of Oregon v. Smith*[21] and in so doing revealed the global character of his objection to constitutional rules that turned on effect. In that case, Scalia denied that the First Amendment, as made applicable to the states by the Fourteenth Amendment, required exceptions for objections advanced by religious groups because of the effect on them of neutral rules of general applicability.

Both *Washington v. Davis* and *Employment Division v. Smith* were foundational for Scalia's jurisprudence. He well understood, however, that both were contested, on and off the Court, and that neither decision had previously been applied to voting. He also understood that, in *Crawford* itself, a clear majority—not just the five who subscribed to the sliding scale balancing test, but also Breyer—refused to extend the principles of those two rulings to voting. Impact matters. Scalia therefore went out of his way in *Crawford* to treat the issue as an original matter and, in so doing, claimed that the approach of the majority "would prove especially disruptive" because it would make states' managerial decisions subject to the outcome of the lawsuit. By way of example, he mentioned a lawsuit challenging the managerial decisions of a state "reducing the number of polling places" or a lawsuit to compel a state to adopt "voting over the Internet or expand absentee balloting."[22]

Implicit in Scalia's charge concerning the disruptive impact of litigation challenging state managerial laws is the notion that elections are time sensitive and that increasing the risks of such litigation would prevent the adherence to the scheduled election. He insisted on clear, ex ante rules. Considering the issue as an original matter, Scalia also objected to the approach of the majority on the ground that it would "flout the Constitution's express commitment of the task to the States," which he defined as one of weighing "the costs and benefits of possible changes to their election codes."[23]

What is missing from Scalia's objections to the sliding scale balancing test, or any other test that allowed would-be voters to get out from under the burden the state imposed on their exercise of the right to vote, is an appreciation of the possibility of minimizing disruption of election schedules by carefully delineating the bounds within which the managerial decisions of the state might be made. A single case may become the occasion for generating an ex ante rule that would govern other elections in other localities. In *Crawford*, the Court was not just making a decision about the November 2008 elections in Indiana but creating national precedent on voter ID laws. Even more importantly, Scalia's attack on the sliding scale balancing test, especially Souter's application of it, does not account for the importance attached to the right to vote within the democratic system of government, which I maintain is the starting point and premise that guided Souter's application of the sliding scale balancing test. Scalia acknowledged the importance the Court had attached to the right to vote by citing, in a footnote, *Harper v. Virginia Board of Elections*, only to brush that decision of the Court aside.

In this footnote, Scalia recognized that *Harper* "strictly scrutinized nondiscriminatory voting laws requiring the payment of fees," but only referred to that decision as one of "our early right-to-vote decisions."[24] One would have thought that in a court of law, the age of a precedent was a reason to respect it, though in this instance Scalia's reference to *Harper*'s date appears more as an effort to disparage its authority. In any event, despite his brief acknowledgment of *Harper*, Scalia, much like Stevens in his opinion, never paused to identify the reason the Court in that case used to justify its ruling setting aside a state law requiring the payment of a tax as condition of voting—the preciousness or fundamentality of the right to vote. *Reynolds v. Sims* was never mentioned.

In a final turn of his argument, Scalia relented. Either to secure the votes of Thomas or more plausibly Alito,[25] or to hold out an olive branch to Stevens, Roberts, or Kennedy, all of whom voted to uphold the Indiana law but applied and thus affirmed their loyalty to the sliding scale balancing test, Scalia introduced a discordant note into his opinion. In a half sentence, he indicated a willingness to set aside a state managerial decision of elections if it "imposes a severe and unjustified overall burden upon the right to vote."[26]

In so doing, Scalia minimized and thus trivialized the difference between his approach and the approach of those who subscribed to the sliding scale balancing test. He reduced that difference to the difference between "serious" and "severe." Under the sliding scale balancing test, the Court would not be confined to curbing "severe" impacts but could also review management decisions that have "serious" adverse impact on the exercise of the right to vote. In such cases, the sliding scale balancing test would adjust downward the character of the burden imposed on the state to justify the measure—the law need not be justified by a "compelling" public purpose, a "significant" or "important" one would suffice.

More fundamentally, Scalia's half-hearted concession strikes me as inconsistent with the broad jurisprudential significance he attributes to *Washington v. Davis* and *Employment Division v. Smith* and his insistence that the approach of the majority would "flout the Constitution's express commitment of the [managerial] task to the states." Scalia's willingness to set aside a "severe" burden on the exercise of the right to vote constitutes a betrayal and thus a mockery of his disdain for paying attention to the effects or social consequences of a law, at least when such an approach is applied to voting. The difference between "serious" and "severe" is surely one of degree, not kind. If a "severe" adverse impact is sufficient to question the law causing it, then it stands to reason that a "serious" adverse impact should also call into question the validity of the law and put the state to the burden of justifying it, though, under the logic of the sliding scale balancing test, the standard for what constitutes an acceptable justification might be less exacting.

THE UNCERTAIN FUTURE OF THE DUTY OF FACILITATION

The significance of *Crawford* and the divisions among the justices should not be underestimated. It was the first occasion that the Court had to examine the state's discharge of its managerial responsibility over elections. It is, at this moment, also the last word of the Court on this subject. In the end, *Crawford* should be read as endorsing the sliding scale balancing test and extending it from the cases reviewing state laws that restrict access to the ballot to cases reviewing the managerial decisions of the states governing elections.

Among the many tests presented in *Crawford*, Souter's application of the sliding scale balancing test, guided as it was by the recognition of the fundamentality of the right to vote, might be taken as a juridical instrument for implementing the duty of facilitation. Arguably, anchoring the duty of facilitation in the right to vote, understood as a constitutional as opposed to simply a fundamental right, might yield a more dynamic understanding of the duty of facilitation. Yet one must avoid making too much out of the difference between a fundamental and a constitutional right.

As a fundamental right, the right to vote is a trigger for strict scrutiny, which is to govern the application of equal protection. In the hands of Souter, it becomes a guide for the application of the sliding scale balancing test, which presumably constitutes yet another test for governing the application of equal protection. As a constitutional right of its own, the right to vote is the right to be applied and protected and, as a result, might, as I just suggested, provide a more forceful and stringent duty of facilitation. Still, even if the right to vote is a constitutional as opposed to a fundamental right, it might call for the very same standard for judging the adequacy of the state law that Souter in fact used. Souter acknowledged that states are entitled to enact measures to prevent fraud and to preserve the integrity of the electoral process but any such measure that hinders the exercise of the right to vote needs to be justified. The burden of justification will vary and, in the end, depend on the seriousness of the hindrance and availability of alternatives that might minimize that hindrance.

Unfortunately, Souter's application and understanding of the sliding scale balancing test only had the support of one other justice, Ruth Bader Ginsburg. Yet that should not belittle its significance. Sometimes a dissent or even a lonely concurrence introduces into the law a strain or perspective that one day may triumph. These opinions appeal to the conscience of the law, and the views expressed in them may soon be embraced by a majority. This was indeed the fate of Holmes's dissents in *Lochner v. New York* (1905) and *Abrams v. United States* (1919) and Brandeis's concurrence in *Whitney v. California* (1927) and his dissent in *Olmstead v. United States* (1928), all of which reveal a truth about the path of the law. The significance of an opinion is not defined by the number of justices who, at the moment it is announced, are prepared to support it.

Viewed from this perspective, I am inclined to celebrate Souter's dissent in *Crawford* because it preserves and gives life to the duty of facilitation—a duty rooted, as it is, not in the jurisprudence of equality but in the promise of freedom arising from the Constitution and its democratic ideal.

CHAPTER 4

. . .

The Equality of Votes

DEMOCRACY AS A system of government and constitutional ideal
has both collective and individual dimensions. The freedom that
it generates by having the ruled choose their rulers belongs to the
people as a people. It is a collective freedom. The requirement of
coextensionality and the duty of facilitation seek to promote this
freedom and thus reflect its collective character. On the other hand,
once the appropriate constitutional bounds are set on the power
of the states to determine the criteria for eligibility to vote and to
manage the electoral process, a vital domain exists in which individualistic values are paramount. It is for individuals to decide how to
cast their votes and, when they do, the governing assumption is that
the vote of one person will count as much as that of another.

This allocation of power to the individual does not deny the collective nature of the freedom that democracy generates, though it
reveals the distinctive character of the collectivity—the people—
that enjoys that freedom. Democracy does not treat the people as
an organic community, as one might regard a family or a clan or a
tribe or even an ethnic group (the *volk*). Rather, it views the people

Why We Vote. Owen Fiss, Oxford University Press. © Owen Fiss 2024.
DOI: 10.1093/oso/9780197746387.003.0005

as a composite of a vast number of individuals who, in choosing their leaders, stand as equals and who are bound together by the political system under which they live. From this perspective, we protect the collective by protecting the individual's right to vote. Each election reconstitutes the collective.

SETTING THE BOUNDARIES OF ELECTORAL DISTRICTS

In June 1964, the Supreme Court handed down its decision in *Reynolds v. Sims* and in so doing gave bold and decisive expression to one of the individual-oriented tenets of democracy—the principle requiring the equality of votes. The case concerned the parameters of the electoral districts that were used by Alabama to choose representatives to the two statewide legislative chambers—a House of Representatives consisting of 106 members and a Senate consisting of 35 members. The boundaries of the electoral districts were set in 1901, when the Alabama Constitution was adopted, and at that time the electoral districts were presumably properly apportioned. Each contained roughly the same number of voters. Over the next sixty years, as people moved from the farms to the cities and their surroundings, the state legislature, due to what was referred to as the "rural strangle," failed or refused to adjust the lines of the electoral districts to reflect the population shifts.

As a result of this impasse, both chambers of the Alabama legislature became controlled by representatives who were, according to the 1960 census, elected by a minority of the statewide electorate. Under the 1901 electoral districting scheme, only 25% of Alabama's total population resided in districts that could elect a majority of the House. The same was true of the Senate. To mention one example, a largely rural county such as Bullock, with a population in 1960 of 13,462, had two electoral districts and thus could send two members to the House. Meanwhile Mobile County, which included the city of Mobile and had a population of 314,301 (nearly 25 times more than Bullock County) could elect only three seats. Jefferson County, which included the city of Birmingham and had a population of 634,864 (nearly 50 times larger than Bullock County), had seven seats. Similar patterns were present in the Senate.

Chief Justice Warren wrote the opinion of the Court in *Reynolds v. Sims*, thereby underscoring its significance for the Court and the country. Justices Tom Clark and Potter Stewart filed very brief concurrences, voicing what may well be seen as nothing more than an expression of their unease or reluctance with the outcome. Only Justice John Harlan filed what might be considered an unqualified dissent and it was a strong one at that. Warren prevailed and, speaking for a solid majority, held that the Alabama districting scheme was unconstitutional. Warren decreed that only a scheme of districting that provided for approximately equal population in each of the electoral districts would satisfy the requirement of the Constitution.

The Court's opinion in *Reynolds v. Sims* is often associated with a rule that proclaims "one person, one vote." But the simplicity of this rule obscures the fact that the Court's decision stemmed from the principle requiring the equality of votes, not people. The standard that emerged from this opinion, requiring approximately equal population in all electoral districts, was only a means for protecting the equality of votes. Warren well understood that the population of one geographically defined electoral district as compared to the others might include an inordinate number of citizens who are not eligible to vote, either because of the presence of a state prison, for example, or the presence of a large number of immigrants who have not yet become citizens. Yet Warren viewed the population of electoral districts as an approximate indication of the number of eligible voters within it. Moreover, thanks to the decennial federal census, which for obvious, pragmatic reasons counts residents, not eligible voters, the equal population standard provides an especially convenient and workable way of measuring the number of would-be voters.

The Chief Justice clearly defined the constitutional wrong of the Alabama districting scheme in terms of the "debasement," "dilution," or "undervaluation" of the votes cast by eligible voters in the more populous electoral districts. He began his analysis with the broadest of postulates. "Undeniably," he said, "the Constitution of the United States protects the right of all qualified citizens to vote, in state as well as in federal elections."[1] He then proceeded to identify an obvious corollary that followed from this postulate, namely, that the Constitution would be violated if "certain otherwise qualified voters had been entirely prohibited from voting for members of their state legislature."[2] Turning to the case at hand, Warren acknowledged that Alabama had not prohibited qualified voters in the more populous electoral districts from voting. Alabama only had, through setting the bounds of electoral districts, reduced the value or weight of the votes once tabulated. For Warren, this was a difference without any significance: reducing the worth or value of a voter—dilution—would be, like a rule prohibiting eligible voters from casting their vote, a violation of the Constitution.

After identifying the constitutional wrong inherent in prohibiting some otherwise qualified voters from casting their ballots, Warren continued:

> And, if a State should provide that the votes of citizens in one part of the State should be given two times, or five times, or 10 times the weight of votes of citizens in another part of the State, it could hardly be contended that the right to vote of those residing in the disfavored areas had not been effectively diluted. It would appear extraordinary to suggest that a State could be constitutionally permitted to enact a law providing that certain of the State's voters could vote two, five, or 10 times for their

legislative representatives, while voters living elsewhere could vote only once. And it is inconceivable that a state law to the effect that, in counting votes for legislators, the votes of citizens in one part of the State would be multiplied by two, five, or 10, while the votes of persons in another area would be counted only at face value, could be constitutionally sustainable. Of course, the effect of state legislative districting schemes which give the same number of representatives to unequal numbers of constituents is identical. Overweighting and overvaluation of the votes of those living here has the certain effect of dilution and undervaluation of the votes of those living there. The resulting discrimination against those individual voters living in disfavored areas is easily demonstrable mathematically. Their right to vote is simply not the same right to vote as that of those living in a favored part of the State. Two, five, or 10 of them must vote before the effect of their voting is equivalent to that of their favored neighbor. Weighting the votes of citizens differently, by any method or means, merely because of where they happen to reside, hardly seems justifiable.[3]

The equality of which Warren spoke in this passage—the crucial one in *Reynolds v. Sims*—is not an equality of influence or an equality of the capacity of various groups, however defined, to elect a candidate of their choice. It is simply the equality of votes among those who are qualified to vote—the vote of one voter is worth as much as that of another. Trying to achieve equalities of another variety among citizens might be a worthy, indeed compelling endeavor. It is not, however, required by democracy understood as a system of government that generates political freedom by having those who are ruled choose their rulers. The equality that *Reynolds v. Sims* vindicates is the equality of democracy, not of equal protection, although

Warren, as a purely formal matter, rested his decision on the Equal Protection Clause.

In 1982, the Voting Rights Act of 1965 was amended to guarantee Blacks and other so called protected groups the right "to elect representatives of their choice." Drawing on the language of a 1973 ruling based on the Fourteenth Amendment,[4] this provision has been used to outlaw state districting practices—some abandoning single-member districts altogether and moving to an at-large system of representatives, others dividing and then distributing the Black community among predominantly white districts—that had the effect of diluting the electoral power of Black communities. The Supreme Court upheld the 1982 amendment in *Thornburg v. Gingles* and turned that law into an instrument for increasing the number of representatives who were Black or who were especially responsive to the socio-economic interests of the Black community.[5] While such a result may be justified on grounds of racial equality, as a remedy for the historic exclusion of Blacks from representative governing bodies or as a means of eradicating the vestiges of the racial caste structure, it does not appear to be compelled by democratic freedom.

In February 1964, only four months before *Reynold v. Sims* was handed down, the Court held unconstitutional the congressional districting scheme of Georgia on the ground that it was malapportioned. Justice Hugo Black wrote the Court's opinion in this case, *Wesberry v. Sanders*, and the Court, as in *Reynolds v. Sims*, was nearly unanimous.[6] Only Justice Harlan fully dissented in *Wesberry*. Mild-mannered, respectful of his colleagues, and deliberate in his ways, Harlan nevertheless began his dissent on a high-pitched note: "I had not expected to witness the day when the Supreme Court of the United States would render a decision which casts grave doubt on the constitutionality of the composition of the House of Representatives."[7] Harlan's dissent in *Reynolds v. Sims* had the same tone.

Writing for the Court in *Wesberry v. Sanders*, Justice Black obviously could not rely on the Equal Protection Clause of the Fourteenth Amendment, as Warren would soon do in *Reynolds v. Sims*, since that provision, by its very terms, applies only to the states. Instead, Black rested his decision on Section 2 of Article I of the Constitution. It provides that "[t]he House of Representatives should be composed of members chosen every second year by the People of the several States." Focusing on the words "by the People," Black found within Section 2 a prohibition on the very same debasement, dilution, and undervaluation of the votes that would soon be condemned by Warren in *Reynolds v. Sims* as a violation of equal protection. As Black put it in *Wesberry v. Sanders*, "the Federal Constitution intends that when qualified voters elect members of Congress each vote be given as much weight as any other vote . . . ."[8] In conclusion, Black required congressional districts to contain, as much as is practicable, equal number of persons, although, like Warren in *Reynolds v. Sims*, he did so on the understanding that equality of population was merely an instrument or pragmatic device for protecting the equality of votes.

In *Reynolds v. Sims*, Warren generously quoted Black's language in *Wesberry v. Sanders*. At the same time, Warren was explicit in acknowledging that *Wesberry v. Sanders* could not be dispositive since the claim in *Reynolds v. Sims* was predicated on the Equal Protection Clause and the claim vindicated in *Wesberry v. Sanders* was predicated on Section 2 of Article I. Yet Warren saw in *Wesberry* a principle or idea of great relevance and importance for *Reynolds*. He framed the question he confronted in *Reynolds v. Sims* as "whether there are any constitutionally cognizable principles which would justify departures from the basic standard of equality among voters in the apportionment of seats in state legislatures."[9]

In the end, the result in *Wesberry v. Sanders* and *Reynolds v. Sims* converged, even though each was predicated on different constitutional provisions, one formulated in 1787 governing the federal House of Representatives and the other in 1868 governing the states and prohibiting them from denying anyone equal protection of the laws. This convergence does not necessarily impeach the rulings in these two cases. It does, however, give one reason to believe that the true basis for these decisions was not the specific textual provisions or fragments of text invoked by the Court but rather democracy, now treated as a guiding ideal of the Constitution. The convergence suggests that the textual provisions invoked in the two cases—the phrase "by the People" and the Equal Protection Clause—function as pegs upon which a basic democratic tenet—requiring the equality of votes—might be hung.

Certainly, the use in Section 2 of Article I of the phrase "by the People," which appears in a provision that speaks directly to the terms of those elected to the House of Representatives, does not on its face require equality of votes with the same degree of stringency as the Court decreed by *Wesberry*. The Court disallowed any significant adjustments to achieve geographic compactness or to enhance the representation of political subdivisions. In summarizing *Wesberry v. Sanders*, Warren said that the phrase "by the People" had been "construed in its historical context."[10] But the reader is left to wonder what was the special historical context to which he was referring. Could it have been the general ambition of the framers to establish a democracy? If so, then that ambition and the decision to make democracy a guiding ideal of the Constitution should be seen as the grounds of the decision, not the phrase "by the People" as it appears in Section 2 of Article I.

The reference to the Equal Protection Clause in *Reynolds v. Sims* also seems contrived. A decade earlier, Warren, once again speaking for the Court, this time in *Brown v. Board of Education*, read the Equal Protection Clause to condemn the Jim Crow educational systems that then prevailed in seventeen states and the District of

Columbia. He concluded that segregated education impaired the quality of educational opportunities of Blacks, thereby perpetuating their subordination and subjugation. This ruling represents one of the most noble and memorable rulings in the history of the Supreme Court, yet it does not yield a principle that could be used to require equality of votes in electoral districts.

By the middle of the twentieth century, the reach of the Equal Protection Clause was broadened. It was not confined to the historical mission of protecting the newly freed slaves. It was also seen, more generally, as prohibiting any arbitrary or capricious action that disadvantaged some persons or groups over others. Offhand, this might be the understanding of equal protection that Warren had in mind when he condemned the electoral districts in Alabama because they, without any good reason, debased, diluted, or undervalued the votes of those who resided in more heavily populated districts.

Yet it is difficult to see how this more expansive understanding of the Equal Protection Clause as a general guarantee of equal treatment could justify Warren's invocation of that clause as the basis for the equal population standard in *Reynolds v. Sims*. That standard was too absolute to serve that purpose. Warren denied that any factor, even a state's desire to create geographically compact districts or to enhance the representation of a political subdivision (for example, a county), would be permissible. Although Warren acknowledged that such factors could be considered in drawing the boundaries of electoral districts, he was also insistent that that these factors would not justify a sacrifice or, perhaps more accurately, a significant sacrifice of the equal population standard and in that way compromise the equality of votes. In insisting upon the equality of population or equality of votes in this way, Warren disallowed state practices that might be arguably justified and, for that reason, could not be condemned as arbitrary or capricious, or as a breach of the general norm requiring a justification for differences in treatment.

[95]

It was of course open at this point for Warren to say, for example, that although the representation of a political subdivision, for example, might be justified, it is not sufficiently justified to warrant a sacrifice of the equal population standard (as a proxy for equality of votes). Such an argumentative strategy would be similar to the one Warren eventually used in *Kramer v. Union Free School District No. 15* (discussed in Chapter 2)—the fundamental rights branch of strict scrutiny. In that case, speaking for the majority, Warren acknowledged that although ownership or property might be deemed a relevant or permissible qualification for voting in a school board election, it was not a compelling one and on that basis concluded that the state law constituted a denial of equal protection.

Such an argument depends on three propositions: (1) the right to vote is a fundamental right; (2) any transgression, even a dilution or undervaluation, imposes a special burden of justification on the state; and (3) any justification for the state's action, for example the desire to give recognition to political subdivisions or to preserve geographic compactness, would not constitute a sufficient justification. The second step is tautological. The other two are not tautological but rather constitute substantive propositions of constitutional law. Formally, however, they were based not on equal protection but, like Black's interpretation of "by the People," on democratic principles.

The first proposition, proclaiming the right to vote as a fundamental right, acknowledges the importance or, if you will, preciousness of the right to vote. As explained in Chapter 1, the importance of the right to vote stems not from its role in furthering the welfare or pragmatic interest of the individual, nor even because, as expressed by some, it is the right that is preservative of all other rights. Instead, the importance or fundamentality of the vote stems from the decisive role it plays in a democratic system. It is the means by which those who are ruled choose their rulers and thus generates the political freedom that democracy promises.

Similarly, the unwillingness of Warren to allow, even for such seemingly worthy goals as providing a measure of representation for political subdivisions or preserving geographical compactness—to justify departures from the equal population rule for electoral district can only be explained by his commitment to a basic individual oriented tenet of democracy—one citizen's vote is as worthy as another's.

By the end of Warren's tenure, as indicated by his decision in the *Kramer* case, the application of the fundamental rights branch of strict scrutiny in cases involving the selective distribution of the franchise became commonplace. Under strict scrutiny, judgments must be made about the worthiness of the public purpose—is it compelling? Arguably, the same kind of judgment is being made in *Reynolds v. Sims*, but to me the judgment implicit in the equal population rule is far more relentless. It says that no public purpose could ever be sufficiently compelling to justify a departure from the equal population rule for electoral districts. Such absolutism could only be based on an attachment to the democratic tenet requiring the equality of votes. It has nothing to do with equal protection. In sum, what I said about *Wesberry v. Sanders* and the use of the phrase "by the People" in Section 2 of Article I must also be said of Warren's use of the Fourteenth Amendment's Equal Protection Clause in *Reynolds v. Sims*—it is formal, legalistic pretext.

In *Reynolds v. Sims*, Warren was careful to preserve the authority of Alabama to divide its legislature into two chambers. Although the desire to give some special representation to political subdivisions or geographic compactness cannot justify sacrifices of the equal population standard in either chamber, the two chambers might be differentiated, Warren explained by way of example, in terms of the number of members or the length of their service. Warren readily acknowledged that the equality of population as a proxy for the equality of votes denied to the state what is allowed to the federal government because the United States Senate contains two representatives from each state. Warren fully understood that this arrangement for the Senate—two senators for each state—violated the principle requiring the equality of votes when the nation is viewed as a whole. Yet he also seemed resolved not to allow it to undermine the effort to fulfill the overall democratic purposes of the Constitution. Wisely, Warren deemed the rule governing representation of states in the Senate an exception that was to be strictly confined.

The Constitution of 1787 provided that the two senators from each state were to be chosen by the legislatures of each state. In 1913, the Constitution was amended to provide for the direct election—by the people—of each senator. That amendment also reaffirmed the original scheme that provided that "the Senate of the United States shall be composed of two senators from each State." In effect, the Constitution, which gave the Senate lawmaking authority over the entire nation, treated each state as an electoral district and, in so doing, it could be said, "debased," "diluted," or "undervalued" the votes of citizens in the more populous states. In strictly numerical terms, the worth of a vote in New York, viewed on an individualistic basis, is significantly less than a vote in Rhode Island.

In his opinion in *Reynolds v. Sims*, Warren acknowledged, as he had to, that the rule requiring equal representation of the states in the Senate violates the principle of the equality of votes. He then went on, however, to qualify that breach of the rule as an aberration "conceived out of compromise and concession."[11] The rule allocating two senators to each state and providing that each senator shall have a single vote in the Senate was not one of the many, somewhat ordinary compromises or concessions that invariably permeate any constitution-making process. It was, in Warren's eyes, a truly Faustian bargain, for it was tied to the very creation of the nation, which required, in Warren's terms, "formerly independent States [to] . . . surrender[] some of their sovereignty in agreeing to join together . . . under one national government."[12] The need and uniqueness of the compromise over the Senate is also manifest, as Warren well understood, in Article V of the Constitution and the procedures it provides for amending the Constitution. Article V requires that any amendment must be approved by three-fourths of the states, and then adds, for good measure, that no amendment can deprive any state without its consent "its equal suffrage in the Senate."

Reynolds v. Sims was one of Warren's proudest achievements. When, however, he stepped down in June 1969, a question then arose as to whether that decision would survive. Richard Nixon, who had, as I already noted, campaigned against many of the recent decisions of the Warren Court, was elected president in the 1968 election and during his time in the White House was able to make four appointments to the Supreme Court (described in Chapter 2). In 1973, one of the new appointees, William Rehnquist, wrote for a majority in a decision that allowed states to confine the right to vote to landowners when the state created an elected body with a "special limited purpose."[13] The election in question was designed to choose the Board of Directors of a body charged with implementing the California Water Code. In doing so, Rehnquist carved out an "exception to the rule laid down in *Reynolds*."[14]

In this same Term, Rehnquist also wrote another decision for the Court that qualified the equal population rule of *Reynolds v. Sims* by drawing a distinction between the states' design of congressional electoral districts and the states' design of electoral districts that would be used for choosing representatives to their own legislature.[15] For the latter, the state was required only to make an "honest and good faith effort to construct districts . . . of equal population" and some variation would be acceptable if based on "rational state policy."[16] Both of these decisions provoked dissents by the stalwarts of the Warren Court still on the bench—Douglas, Brennan, and Marshall.

Eventually, these assaults on *Reynolds v. Sims* subsided. In 1989, soon after Rehnquist was named Chief Justice, the Court required the apportionment of a distinctly local body, the Board of Estimate of New York City, and in so doing reaffirmed the core principles of *Reynolds v. Sims*.[17] Rehnquist was, in this instant, in the majority and assigned the responsibility of writing for the majority to Justice White, who, in 1964, had joined Warren's opinion in *Reynolds v. Sims*. White's opinion garnered the support of Marshall, though Brennan wrote a separate concurrence. Accordingly, in 1989, *Reynolds v. Sims* and its rule requiring equality of votes appeared bruised, now subject to the limitations imposed on it by the Court in the 1970s, but in the end, it remained good law. As White wrote in the Board of Estimate case, "the Court has insisted that seats in legislative bodies be apportioned to districts of substantially equal populations."[18]

TABULATING THE VOTES

Reynolds v. Sims was predicated on the premise that the outright denial of the votes of people who are qualified to vote is a constitutional wrong. *Reynolds* extended that principle to the dilution or undervaluation of votes. In the December 2000 decision of *Bush v. Gore*,[19] the alleged wrong arose not from the construction of electoral districts but rather from the application, by administrative officials, of different standards for determining which votes should be counted and which ones disallowed. The technical legal issue in the case was mundane. It consisted of a challenge to the method being used to tabulate votes. But the public's interest in the case grew to extravagant proportions because the outcome of the November 2000 presidential election turned on it.

Soon after the polls were closed, the Secretary of State of Florida ruled that George W. Bush had won the popular vote of the state. The margin of his victory was extremely narrow. The Secretary said that Bush had won by 1,178 votes out of the more than 6 million votes cast. Mindful of the narrow margin, the Supreme Court of Florida ordered a recount and, on December 12, the Supreme Court of the United States stopped that recount. The U.S. Supreme Court ruling left in effect the order of the Florida Secretary of State declaring that Bush had won the popular vote in Florida. As a result, Bush was awarded Florida's 25 electoral votes, which secured his victory in the Electoral College (even though he lost the popular vote viewed on a national basis).

Florida had used two different methods for tabulating votes, depending on the county: optical scanners and punch cards. The recount was aimed at those counties that had used punch cards. Some voters had not fully or properly perforated the card with the stylus they were given and, as a result, the machines reading those cards did not register a vote for one of the candidates, even though the intent of the voter might have been clear. In some instances, the piece of cardboard indicating the voter's preference—referred to as a chad—might have been indented or dimpled but was not fully pushed through the card. Or, even if the punch card had been perforated, the chad remained hanging on the card by two corners. Under either of these circumstances, the machine reading the punch cards would not record a vote for any candidate, though the intent of the voter was clear. It was estimated that some 60,000 ballots were subject to this failure of the punch card voting system. The Supreme Court of Florida ordered that the ballots in question be subject to a manual recount.

The Florida court directed that votes should be tallied by canvassing teams only if the punch card contained a clear indication of the voter's intent. The Florida court did not, however, announce a subsidiary set of rules that would indicate with some specificity what should be done with, for example, the dimpled or hanging chads in determining the clear intent of the voter. As a result, there was a considerable risk that the manual hand count could lead to disparities—one dimpled chad might be tabulated, another would not. This risk might well be magnified by the multitude of individuals, spread through a number of different counties, who would be responsible for inspecting the punch cards and making a judgment of whether the intent of the voter was clear enough to justify tabulating a vote for one candidate as opposed to the other. Although the risk of such disparities was tempered by the fact that any objection to the work of the canvassing teams conducting the manual recount could be resolved in various state circuit courts and, if need be, by the Supreme Court of Florida, the danger of unequal treatment of individual votes posed by the manual recount persisted.

The U.S. Supreme Court was divided five to four. One of the dissenters, David Souter, cut to the core. Much as he later did in the photo ID case (Chapter 3), Souter acknowledged the legacy of *Reynolds v. Sims* and its progeny and began his analysis by recognizing the fundamental nature of the right to vote. Accordingly, he was troubled by the risk that the manual recount posed to the equality of votes and the threat to equal protection. He said, "I can conceive of no legitimate state interest served by these differing treatments of the expressions of voters' fundamental rights."[20] Yet he dissented from the judgment of his Court setting aside the order of the Florida court ordering the recount. He believed that the proper remedy was not for the Supreme Court of the United States to stop the manual recount. Rather, he thought the Supreme Court of the United States should remand the case to the Florida Supreme Court with instructions that the Florida court should develop the subsidiary rules for conducting the recount, thereby minimizing the danger to the principle requiring equality of votes.

There was a question as to whether there was adequate time for this remand. The case was argued on December 11 and the Court's decision was issued on December 12. December 18 was the date set by federal statute on which the electors had to meet in Florida to cast their votes in accordance with the popular vote. Conceivably, the subsidiary rules Souter contemplated could be formulated and implemented in the period between December 12 and 18. A problem arose, however, since the Florida legislature had previously indicated that it wanted to take advantage of the safe harbor provisions of a federal statute. To secure that advantage the popular vote had to be certified by the secretary of state on December 12, the very day the Supreme Court handed down its decision.

The safe harbor statute provides that if a dispute over the electoral votes of the state should erupt when the two houses of Congress meet to tabulate the electoral votes, Congress is obliged to accept the votes of the electors of the state that are certified by the governor, provided the certification occurs by December 12. The Florida Supreme Court had decided, however, not to allow the state legislature's desire to take advantage of the safe harbor provision to take priority over the state law that required a recount in cases where the popular vote appeared exceedingly close. Better to forgo the safe harbor protection, the Florida court reasoned, than to choose electors when serious doubts persist about the outcome of the popular vote. On this reading of the Florida court's decision, it therefore seemed that there was still time for Justice Souter's suggested remand.

The majority's reason for rejecting Souter's logic is not clear, in part because the majority itself was divided in two. Five justices voted to stop the recount and these five subscribed to an opinion labeled "Per Curiam" supporting that judgment. In the past, that label was primarily used to announce orders under the Court's summary doctrine or to justify ministerial orders over which there was no division. In *Bush v. Gore*, however, there was sharp division, even among the five justices who supported the judgment, so the label was probably intended to minimize the appearance of division among the majority.

Yet this patina of agreement was remarkably thin. Although three of the five justices—Rehnquist, Scalia, and Thomas—said, very briefly, that they subscribed to the Per Curiam they went on to sign another opinion—this one written by Rehnquist—that did not overlap in any way with that of the Per Curiam. I thus think it is fair to say that Rehnquist and the two other justices who subscribed to his opinion did not have their heart in the Per Curiam. I thus read the Per Curiam as essentially setting forth the reasons that Justices Kennedy and O'Connor offered to support their decisions to stop the recount ordered by the Florida Supreme Court.

In the Per Curiam, Kennedy and O'Connor complained of the absence of standards to guide the recount. In the end, they acknowledged that the risk of disparities in the tabulating processes could be corrected by the issuance of subsidiary standards by the Florida Supreme Court. Unlike Souter, however, they thought there was not sufficient time for the Florida Court to promulgate these standards. Their eyes were on the statutory safe harbor date—December 12— and they denied the Florida Supreme Court the authority to make the judgment that achieving a correct count of the popular vote in Florida was more important than taking advantage of the safe harbor that federal law provided for the tabulation.

Kennedy and O'Connor primarily based their objection to the risk of disparities on equal protection, much like Souter. Yet at times they also expressed the view that this risk of disparities constituted a violation of due process. The Per Curiam began with the announcement that the case presented the question of "whether the use of standardless manual recounts violates the Equal Protection and Due Process Clauses."[21] Later, after describing the complexity of the manual recount, the Per Curiam stated: "Upon due consideration of the difficulties identified to this point, it is obvious that the recount cannot be conducted in compliance with the requirements of equal protection and due process without substantial additional work."[22] In a similar vein, the Per Curiam invoked one of the central hallmarks of due process when it characterized the recount as a denial of "fundamental fairness." The opinion reads: "When a court orders a statewide remedy, there must be at least some assurance that the rudimentary requirements of equal protection and fundamental fairness are satisfied."[23]

Any exercise of a discretionary power by a state agency entails the risk of disparities. We must then ask why the risk of disparities in the recount process, as opposed to the risk of disparities inherent in, for example, welfare, police, and education services, should constitute a violation of equal protection. Even for due process, there is an obvious need for some limiting principle. Souter found that limiting principle in the fundamentality of voting in a democratic society. Although Kennedy and O'Connor made a gesture in the same direction, in the end, they stopped short of Souter's acknowledging the fundamentality of the right to vote.

Kennedy and O'Connor cited *Harper v. Virginia Board of Elections*, one of the most famous progeny of *Reynolds v. Sims*, and which had in turn embraced Warren's characterization in *Reynolds* of the fundamentality of the right to vote. In contrast to Souter, however, Kennedy and O'Connor significantly qualified their recognition of voting as a fundamental right when they made fundamentality dependent on recognition by the state. As the Per Curiam reads:

> When the state legislature vests the right to vote for President in its people, the right to vote as a legislature has proscribed is fundamental; and one source of its fundamental nature lies in

the equal weight accorded to each vote and the equal dignity owed to each voter.

In making the fundamentality of the right to vote dependent upon a decision of the state legislature, Kennedy and O'Connor inverted the function of fundamentality. As *Harper* made clear, the fundamental character of the right to vote provides the grounds for judging the adequacy of a state law setting the qualifications for voting and thus cannot be made dependent on whether the state decides to honor or vest the right to vote. Granted, democracy requires equality of votes, but this equality is not the source, but rather the consequence of recognizing the fundamental character of the right to vote.

Justice Rehnquist had no taste for "fundamental fairness" as a constitutional norm. Nor did he have much taste for the view that regarded voting as a fundamental right. Arguably, the same could be said of Scalia and Thomas. Soon after Rehnquist began his career on the Court, he sought ways to avoid acknowledging the fundamental character of voting. As we saw in Chapter 2, in the 1974 *Richardson v. Ramirez* decision, Rehnquist used Section 2 of the Fourteenth Amendment to avoid recognition of the fundamentality of voting that so animated Thurgood Marshall's dissent in that case. In *Bush v. Gore*, Rehnquist used Article II for the same purpose, though in this instance perhaps to avoid the thin and confused recognition of the fundamentality of voting that appeared in the Per Curiam penned by Kennedy and O'Connor.

Section 1 of Article II governs the election of the president. Clause 2 of Section 1 specifies the manner of selecting the members of the Electoral College. It provides:

> Each State shall appoint, in such Manner as the Legislature thereof may direct, a Number of Electors, equal to the whole Number of Senators and Representatives to which the State may

be entitled in the Congress: but no Senator or Representative, or Person holding an Office of Trust or Profit under the United States, shall be appointed an Elector.

This provision is aimed primarily at setting the number of electors for each state and precluding certain officials from serving as electors. The mention of state legislatures is wholly incidental. It thus seems contrived to construe this provision of Article II—in the way that Rehnquist did—as a grant of authority for the Supreme Court of the United States to set aside a decision of the Florida Supreme Court that interprets Florida electoral law to require a recount. As Justice Stevens stressed in his dissent, nothing in Article II frees the state legislature from the state constitution that had created it nor does it lessen the authority of the Florida Supreme Court to construe all the provisions of state law, including the state constitution and the laws governing elections. It did not endow the Florida Legislature with a measure of independence from review by the Florida Supreme Court on the meaning of state law.

In an act of desperation, Rehnquist invoked the authority of a ruling of the Supreme Court of the United States that was handed down in 1964, in the heat of the civil rights struggle.[24] In an opinion written by Justice Brennan, in that case the Court set aside an interpretation of a state trespass law by the South Carolina Supreme Court, which had, contrary to an earlier ruling it had rendered, held that the state trespass law applied to Black demonstrators who initially had consent to enter private property but who were then asked to leave. Brennan emphasized the conflict with the earlier interpretation of the trespass law that the South Carolina court rendered and deemed that switch a denial of due process.

In *Bush v. Gore*, there was no switch by the Florida Supreme Court. Nor was there any overriding constitutional mission that could be used to justify the decision in *Bush v. Gore* to set aside the

Florida Supreme Court's interpretation of state law. There was no basis whatsoever for Rehnquist to claim that "the Florida Supreme Court's interpretation of the Florida election laws impermissibly distorted them beyond what a fair reading required, in violation of Article II."[25]

To bolster this conclusion, Rehnquist also invoked the authority of the federal safe harbor statute, referred to as Section 5, claiming that it "informs our application of Art. II."[26] Quite frankly, it is hard to see this statute as providing any support to Rehnquist's use of Article II to deny the authority of the Florida Supreme Court to be the final arbiter of Florida election laws. As Justice Stevens put it, "Section 5, like Article II, assumes the involvement of the state judiciary in interpreting state election laws and resolving election disputes under those laws."[27] Section 5 only sets conditions for treating a state's certification as conclusive in the event that a dispute over those elections needs to be resolved in the Congress. Conclusiveness only requires certification under a legal scheme in place before the election, with results determined at least six days before the date set for casting electoral votes in the state.

The decision in *Bush v. Gore* left a cloud, now perhaps only of historic significance, over the legitimacy of the Supreme Court.[28] Indeed, Justice Breyer warned of such an injury to the authority of the Court in his dissent. Although Breyer, like Souter, acknowledged the need to promulgate subsidiary standards to guide the manual recount, Souter had based his demand for these subsidiary rules on a recognition of the right to vote as a fundamental right. Breyer relied on a lesser standard, what he called "the need of procedural fairness." Breyer thus was able to downgrade the wrong that the majority was seeking to correct and therefore distinguished *Bush v. Gore* from a case involving a principle as foundational as that involved in *Brown v. Board of Education*. Speaking of the majority ruling in

[108]

Bush v. Gore, Breyer said, "the Court is not acting to vindicate a fundamental constitutional principle."[29]

This characterization about the majority's decision enabled Breyer to enter a deeply felt plea for the passive virtues—"judicial restraint"—whenever the Court is "resolving political disputes."[30] This plea for restraint became all the more urgent because the justices knew in advance and with near absolute certainty the result of the action the majority was about to take. The political ramification of the Court's intervention was manifest. Setting aside the order of the Florida Supreme Court requiring a manual recount would result in the election of one presidential candidate over another. They knew that victory would go to the Republican candidate George W. Bush rather than Al Gore, the Democrat.

The willingness of the majority to set aside the action of the Florida Supreme Court also seemed inconsistent with the long and clear pattern of decisions the Supreme Court had rendered since the 1970s, first under the Chief Justiceship of Warren Burger and then under William Rehnquist, calling for greater deference toward state courts. In fact, each of the justices who formed a majority in *Bush v. Gore* repeatedly sought to place limits on the power of the federal courts, through the writ of habeas corpus, to review state criminal convictions. They also set aside federal court injunctions against ongoing criminal and civil proceedings and expanded the reach of the Eleventh Amendment limitation on the jurisdiction by the federal courts over the states. Justified in terms of "Our Federalism," they insisted that federal courts should respect state courts.

Against this background, the need for strong, clear justification for the action of the majority became all the more urgent and on this score they failed miserably. Rehnquist's invocation of Article II was utterly unconvincing. As Stevens politely remarked, it was "not substantial." In fact, eventually the Court repudiated the position of Rehnquist that insulated the work of the Florida legislature from interpretation and review by the Florida Supreme Court.[31] The Florida legislature is a creation of the Florida constitution, and according to that very same constitution, the Florida Supreme Court is, on issues of state law, the final arbiter.

The opinion of Kennedy and O'Connor—set forth in the Per Curiam—was closer to the mark than Rehnquist's. Yet it also failed because Kennedy and O'Connor qualified the conception of fundamentality in such a way as to render it incoherent. They also failed to explain why the risk of disparities in the hand recount could not be adequately curbed by the promulgation of subsidiary rules to ascertain the intent of the voters. Although Kennedy and O'Connor claimed there was no time for such a remedy, Souter convincingly explained why that particular judgment was flawed.

The failure of the majority of five to adequately justify their decisions only magnified the doubts about the legitimacy of the Court's intervention that so worried Breyer. The opinions of the five, however, did not cast any doubt upon the continued validity of *Reynolds v. Sims* and the democratic principle it vindicated, though in a different context, requiring the equality of votes. The Court in *Bush v. Gore* began with the assumption of the equality of votes in place and left it in place. Oddly enough, some might even see in this unfortunate and especially notorious exercise of judicial power an acquiescence as well as a weak affirmation of the principle requiring equality of votes. You can only complain about the risk of disparities if you believe that the votes to be recounted must be treated equally.

CHAPTER 5

. . .

The Constraints of the Ballot

VOTING IS A limited discursive experience. It is not a conversation about who should rule nor a discussion about the policies that would best serve the public interest. It is not a statement of the voters' views or the reasons for their beliefs. In the modern age, voting consists of a choice among the candidates appearing on a ballot or, if a system of preferential voting is used, voting allows citizens to indicate their preferences among the limited number of candidates appearing on the ballot.

The limited nature of the discursive experience of voting can be justified, at least when dealing with a vast multitude of voters, as we inevitably do these days, by the practical purpose of democratic elections, which is to identify, in some expeditious and easily tabulated manner, the individuals who will assume the reins of government. Accordingly, turning the experience of voting into a choice among a limited number of candidates might be seen as a pragmatic necessity. Even so, a judge charged with the duty of implementing the democratic ideal of the Constitution must carefully scrutinize state laws that determine who will appear on the official ballot. The

Why We Vote. Owen Fiss, Oxford University Press. © Owen Fiss 2024.
DOI: 10.1093/oso/9780197746387.003.0006

freedom of voters to choose those who will rule is constrained by the list of names on the ballot, and thus the capacity of an election to generate the political freedom that democracy promises depends on the sources and severity of those constraints.

A reference to the constitutional arrangement in Iran makes the need for such scrutiny abundantly clear. Iran is largely governed by a Supreme Leader who is chosen by a select group of religious scholars—nothing democratic about that process. Yet the country also has an elected president and a parliament and for that reason claims a measure of democratic legitimacy. It purports to be a republic. This claim is in part impaired by the limits the constitution of Iran imposes on the powers of the president and parliament and the fact that it reserves for the Supreme Leader control over the military and judiciary. Even more fundamentally, the capacity of the elections of the president and members of parliament to generate the freedom that belongs to democracy is denied by the Supreme Leader's control over those who are, in his eyes, deemed "qualified" to run for these offices. The Supreme Leader picks and chooses the candidates who are allowed to run for elected offices depending on their loyalty and submissiveness to his policies or dictates—a radical betrayal of the elemental promise of democracy, which extends to the people the right to choose their rulers.

Obviously, there is no Supreme Leader in the United States. The power to determine who may run for office is vested in the legislatures of the various states. As such, the power over who appears on the ballot is decentralized and further limited by the fact that this power must be exercised through the enactment of general rules, not through a system that allows ad hoc approval of candidates by a member of the executive branch. State legislative control over the candidacy of persons running for the House of Representatives and the Senate is derived from Article I of the Constitution. It gives the states the power to manage these elections. Article II also gives the state legislatures the power to determine who are to be the electors in the Electoral College and is understood to vest state legislatures with the power to establish the general rules for determining who appears on the ballot in presidential elections. The power of state legislatures to set the rules for the election of state officials derives from the state constitutions, subject to the same federal constitutional constraints that apply to the election of federal officials.

The American scheme for distributing the power to determine who may run for office lessens the danger to political freedom that might be posed by a system such as the one in the Islamic Republic of Iran. It does not, however, eliminate that danger altogether. It is possible that the members of a state legislature, or a majority of them, most of whom are likely to be members of either the Democratic or Republican party, may enact rules that would protect themselves or their political parties from competition by still other political parties or independent candidates. Although democracy does not require eliminating all rules that have the effect of fencing out challengers, it does require what I will call "feasible access" for these contenders.

Admittedly, an election can generate the political freedom that democracy promises even if only one candidate decides to run for office, or even if a number of candidates are from one of the two major parties that controls the state legislature. An election cannot serve its purpose, however, if the state legislature does not provide feasible access for contenders, either as representatives of new or third parties or as independent candidates, to appear on the ballot and thus challenge the position of the parties that control and dominate the state legislature.

Confining an election to a choice between two candidates, one from the Republican and one from the Democratic party, guarantees that the winning candidate will, in a winner-take-all race, secure a majority of the votes. Accordingly, a rule making it feasible for third parties or independent candidates to run creates a risk—and it is only a risk—that the winner will not secure a majority of those voting. Nevertheless, a constitutional rule requiring feasible access for contenders may have the effect of increasing the number of people who vote and will, even if that does not materialize, enlarge the capacity of an election to achieve its democratic purpose—to provide an opportunity for those who are ruled to choose their rulers. In a winner-take-all system, a run-off between the leading contenders can be used to make certain that the candidate who wins the election secures a majority of the votes cast, assuming that goal is worthy or especially important. Granted, run-offs add expenses and have other drawbacks. Still, from democracy's perspective, it would be better to suffer those inconveniences than to allow a state legislature, in the name of making sure the winner of an election has the support of the majority of those voting, to allow the two dominant parties to insulate themselves from competition.[1]

BEGINNINGS

The rule requiring feasible access for contenders received its first and most dramatic endorsement from the Supreme Court in October 1968, during the run-up to the presidential election of 1968 and the closing days of the Chief Justiceship of Earl Warren.

In March 1968, the then incumbent President Lyndon B. Johnson, facing growing hostility to the country's role in the war in Vietnam, decided not to run for reelection. In thus confronting the ever-increasing risk that the victor of the 1968 presidential election might be Richard Nixon, an outspoken critic of the Court, Warren tendered his resignation to Johnson. The President, in turn, formulated plans to elevate Justice Abe Fortas to the Chief Justiceship and to fill the vacancy created by Warren's retirement with a circuit judge from Texas named Homer Thornberry—who, recall, once made a cameo appearance in Douglas's opinion in *Harper v. Virginia Board of Elections*.[2] Soon enough, these plans were derailed because of financial improprieties of Fortas, and as a result, Warren's resignation, which was to become effective as soon as a successor was appointed, was put on hold. Then, in October 1968, only a month before the November presidential election, the Supreme Court, with Earl Warren presiding, heard arguments in a case—*Williams v. Rhodes*—challenging the constitutionality of Ohio's law governing access to the ballot. A week later, the Court handed down its decision.[3]

Standing on the shoulders of the 1964 decision in *Reynolds v. Sims* and the 1966 decision in *Harper v. Virginia Board of Elections*, the Court's ruling in *Williams v. Rhodes* gave decisive force to the requirement of feasible access. The Court found that Ohio had unconstitutionally constructed a scheme that meant, as a practical matter, that only the Democratic and Republican candidates (Johnson's Vice President Hubert Humphrey and Richard Nixon) would appear on the ballot. By way of remedy, the Court required Ohio to include on the ballot the name of George Wallace. Previously, Wallace had served as governor of Alabama and, in that capacity, achieved great prominence, or better yet, notoriety, when he espoused segregationist views and used his office to prevent the implementation of *Brown v. Board of Education*. He had famously stood in the proverbial schoolhouse door to block Black students from entering schools traditionally designated for whites. In January 1968, Wallace took his cause to the nation and for that purpose formed the American Independent Party.

Due to the fortuity of a number of circumstances, which the Court certainly understood, Wallace's candidacy came at an especially vulnerable time for the Civil Rights Movement. Protests against the Vietnam War had begun to eclipse that movement and, in the spring of 1968, two national figures who, each in his own way, gave that movement purpose and direction were killed. In April,

Martin Luther King Jr. was assassinated in Memphis, Tennessee, and two months later, Robert Kennedy was assassinated in Los Angeles, California. At that time, Kennedy was a U.S. Senator from New York and, as an outspoken critic of the Vietnam War, was the leading contender for Democratic presidential nominee. In early 1960, he had served as the Attorney General of the United States and, in that position, played a leading role in turning the federal government into a vital force for the progressive attainment of racial equality. He had, so to speak, removed Wallace from the school-house door.

The larger purpose of the Court's intervention in *Williams v. Rhodes* and the significance of the circumstances surrounding Wallace's candidacy may be revealed by focusing on a less-remembered feature of the case. There were not one but two so-called third parties seeking access to the ballot—the American Independent Party and the Socialist Labor Party—and the Court only gave access to the first, Wallace's party. The Socialist Labor Party received only ambiguously defined "declaratory relief." Presumably, that relief consisted of a declaration that the Ohio electoral scheme was, in its entirety, unconstitutional. Alternatively, the Court might have contemplated that its declaration of invalidity was aimed only at the provision of the Ohio electoral law that kept the Socialist Labor Party off the ballot—the requirement that it get 15% of the vote in the previous gubernatorial election (the two major parties need only get 10% of that vote). Either way, the Court refused to give the Socialist Labor Party the relief it gave the American Independent Party, which consisted of an order directing the Ohio authorities to include the American Independent Party's candidate—George Wallace—on the presidential ballot.

Justice Hugo Black delivered the opinion of the Court and justified the distinction between the two parties in terms of the lateness of the hour. The case was argued in the Supreme Court on

October 7, 1968, and the Court's opinion was filed on October 15, 1968, very much with an eye on the forthcoming election in the first week of November. In that context, Black, addressing the claim of the Socialist Labor Party, said, "Certainly at this late date it would be extremely difficult, if not impossible, for Ohio to provide still another set of ballots."[4] It is hard to understand, however, why the ballots that had to be amended to include the American Independent Party could not also be revised to include the Socialist Labor Party.

Justice Black would have us believe that this distinction was attributable to the momentary lapse of the lawyers for the Socialist Labor Party. Although the lawyers for the American Independent Party immediately sought and obtained from the circuit justice (Justice Potter Stewart) a stay of the federal district court order that had denied both parties a place on the ballot, the lawyers for the Socialist Labor Party did not immediately seek the same relief from the Court. A few days lapsed before they did so, and at that point Stewart declined to grant their request. I do not understand, however, why Stewart's denial of the stay for the Socialist Labor Party at that stage would justify the eventual decision by the Supreme Court, when it turned to the merits, to deny the Socialist Labor Party the very same relief that it provided, over Stewart's dissent, to the American Independent Party.

A more plausible explanation for the distinction between the two parties' treatment might be found in the history of these parties and the special political significance of Wallace's candidacy in 1968. As the Court acknowledged, the Socialist Labor Party was an old party and a very small one. It had been on the ballot in many states for many years. In fact, it was on the ballot in Ohio until 1948, at which time the state's electoral laws were tightened. The Socialist Labor Party had only 108 members.

In contrast, the American Independent Party was a new party. It was formed by George Wallace in January 1968, with the aim of challenging the position taken by both major parties—the Democrats and the Republicans—on the issue of desegregation and racial equality. Over the next six months, Wallace's supporters managed to obtain 450,000 signatures to place his name on the ballot. (Only 433,000 signatures were needed to meet the required 15% of those who voted in the preceding gubernatorial election.) The Court well understood that to deny Wallace and the American Independent Party a place on the ballot would impair the democratic legitimacy of the 1968 presidential election and deny that election the capacity to generate political freedom. Justice Black described the American Independent Party as "clamoring"[5] for a place on the ballot with a political urgency not possessed by the Socialist Labor Party, at least not in 1968.

Admittedly, even without Wallace on the ballot, the voters in Ohio were able to choose between the Republican and Democratic candidates. These voters would have a choice, but the constraints on their choice were manifest. Black described the electoral laws that privileged the two established parties and placed onerous burdens on third or new parties as creating a "monopoly." As Black put it, the Ohio electoral system did not just favor a two-party system, but rather that it favored "two particular parties—the Republicans and the Democrats—and in effect tends to give them a complete monopoly."[6]

Justice Black's characterization of the power of the two established parties as "a complete monopoly" is a bit of an exaggeration. Both parties had heterogeneous memberships and competed with one another. However, in a system where winner takes all, the competition by the two parties, both in terms of their candidates and the policies they espouse, tended to converge toward the center, with an eye to obtaining the support of what has been referred to as the "median voter." Such a dynamic has its virtues, but these are not virtues prized by democracy, nor do they compensate for the impairment of choice inherently imposed by a ballot.

Ultimately, in the election of November 1968, Wallace received 467,495 votes, well behind Richard Nixon's 1,791,014 votes and Hubert Humphrey's 1,700,586. Yet the decree of the Court placing Wallace, the declared enemy of *Brown*, on the ballot endowed the 1968 presidential election with an integrity that it would not have had without him. The people of Ohio had spoken. The failure to include the Socialist Labor Party did not undermine or contradict that claim. The "people," those who are blessed with the political freedom generated by democracy, is a collectivity. Accordingly, the entitlement of a political party to appear on the ballot necessarily entails an assessment, of the kind the justices made, about the vitality and strength of the support that party can muster in the body politic. The requirement of feasible access applies only to viable contenders. Rooted in the democratic ideal, it seeks to protect the electorate, not the candidates.[7]

As a general matter, challengers to the dominant or hegemonic position of the Republican and Democratic parties may present themselves as independents or as candidates sponsored by third parties. At the time of *Williams v. Rhodes*, Ohio did not allow independent candidates, nor did Wallace present himself as one. He only claimed the right to represent a new party. Under the Ohio scheme, a new party had to obtain the signatures consisting of 15% of the ballots cast in the last gubernatorial election. It also had to file a petition for status as a new party in February of the election year and then, later that year, hold a primary election that would select the candidates of the party and still later choose the members of the party's executive committee and the delegates to the national convention.

Although the American Independent Party had sufficient signatures to meet the 15% requirement for new parties, these signatures were filed in June, not February 1968 as the law required. Fully aware of this failure, the Ohio Secretary of State rejected the signatures as untimely and, accordingly, no primary election was held. The Supreme Court in *Williams v. Rhodes* found the Ohio arrangements for new parties unconstitutional, and it ordered that the party's candidates be given a place on the Ohio ballot. In so doing, the Court treated Wallace and his running mate as de facto independent candidates.

In judging their impact on the American Independent Party, Black reviewed the Ohio electoral laws governing new parties in their entirety. He concluded that these laws denied the party feasible access to the ballot and, furthermore, that they did not serve any public interest that might have justified this infringement on the rights of Ohio voters. As a purely formal matter, Black rested the Court's judgment on the Equal Protection Clause of the Fourteenth Amendment and invoked the so-called fundamental rights branch of strict scrutiny. This test requires the state, whenever it denies or infringes a fundamental right, to show that the contested law is necessary for the attainment of a compelling public purpose.

What was the fundamental right infringed by Ohio? In answering this question, Black said that the Ohio laws governing the ballots "place burdens on two different, although overlapping, kinds of rights—the right of individuals to associate for the advancement of political beliefs, and the right of qualified voters, regardless of their political persuasion, to cast their votes effectively."[8] Justice Black then continued, "Both of these rights, of course, rank among our most precious freedoms."[9]

Soon after identifying freedom of association as precious or fundamental, Black reported that the Court had recently held that freedom of association was protected by the First Amendment guarantee of free speech. He did not pause to explain, however, the relationship between these two categories of rights—fundamental rights and constitutional rights. Are fundamental rights a subcategory of constitutional rights? If so, what distinguishes fundamental rights from the larger category of constitutional rights? Is it simply a matter of importance? Must a fundamental right also be a constitutional right or are there some fundamental rights, at least for our purposes, that are simply a trigger for strict scrutiny, not constitutional rights?

Black left these questions unanswered, even unexplored. In any event, one may safely and fully acknowledge that freedom of association is a constitutional right and also a fundamental right without conceding that Ohio's law denies that freedom. The Ohio law did not criminalize membership in the American Independent Party or especially disadvantage such membership. The law only specified the conditions for a new party to obtain a position on the ballot. Denying a new party feasible access to the ballot may discourage the formation of a new party by lessening the incentives for such organizational activity. Such an effect, however, was of an entirely different character than the consequences the Court sought to guard against in *NAACP v. Button*, which had established the constitutional status of the freedom of association as a necessary implication of the First Amendment.[10] Decided in the heat of the civil rights struggle, *NAACP v. Button* had set aside a law of Alabama that required disclosure of the members of the NAACP because it would expose them to harassment and thus interfere with their freedom to join together in an effort to effectuate political change.

After referring to the right to political association, Black invoked the right of voters "to cast their votes effectively,"[11] which he then used as another ground triggering strict scrutiny and applying the fundamental rights branch of equal protection. Like freedom of association, Justice Black claimed that the right of voters "to cast their votes effectively" was not only "a precious freedom" but also a constitutionally protected freedom. In this instance, the precedent he cited to support this conclusion—*Wesberry v. Sanders* (1964)—was thin. *Wesberry* construed Article I of the Constitution and its provision that the members of the House of Representatives be elected "by the People" to require congressional districts contain approximately equal numbers of voters.[12]

Standing on its own, however, Black's reference to a "right to cast a vote effectively" is problematic, for it is not at all clear what this right might entail or how Ohio interfered with it. In speaking of the right to cast a vote effectively, Black might have had in mind the right of the members or supporters of the American Independent Party to vote for their candidate, for that right would be denied because their candidate would not be on the ballot. Yet such a view obscures the larger significance of the restrictive electoral laws of Ohio. These laws restricted the choices of all the voters of Ohio, not simply the members or supporters of the American Independent Party.

To my mind, the objection to the Ohio scheme arises not from the fact that it interferes with the right of the Ohio electorate to cast their votes effectively, but rather because it deprives their votes of the meaning attributed to them in a democratic system of government. Elections only generate the freedom that democracy promises if the voters are allowed to choose those they wish to govern. Although the choices of the voters may be limited to the candidates appearing on the ballots, such a constraint is compatible with the capacity of the election to generate political freedom only if all viable candidates have feasible access to the ballot. Moreover, the right to cast a meaningful vote, in contrast to Black's right to cast an effective vote, is significantly more than a trigger of strict scrutiny. It is derived from the democratic purposes of the Constitution and as such acts as an independent constraint on the law-making power of Ohio.

Justice Douglas filed a separate opinion in *Williams v. Rhodes.* At the outset of this opinion, he announced that he joined Black's opinion, although in truth his views differed significantly from those of Black and came closer to the mark. Douglas disavowed any reliance on the Equal Protection Clause and its strict scrutiny test. Douglas's objection to the Ohio scheme was based entirely on the First Amendment. As he declared, "The First Amendment, made applicable to the States by reason of the Fourteenth Amendment, lies at the root of these cases."[13]

Justice Douglas well understood that, by its terms, the First Amendment guaranteed the freedom of speech. Yet he saw that guarantee as the source of a number of other constitutional rights— necessary implications. One such right was the right of association. Justice Black had invoked this right but, for Douglas, at least in *Williams v. Rhodes*, it was not a trigger of strict scrutiny (which he dismissed as just another balancing test). The right of free association was instead, perhaps like any other constitutional right, a direct, independent constraint on the exercise of state power. Douglas also saw the First Amendment as a source of the right to vote. In contrast to Black, however, Douglas spoke of a right to vote (with no modification—Black spoke only of a right to cast a vote effectively) and viewed that right as he did any constitutional right (including the right to free association)—not as a trigger for protecting another constitutional right, such as equal protection. The right to vote, for Douglas, was a direct, independent constraint on state power. Summarizing his position, Douglas wrote: "Cumbersome election machinery can effectively suffocate the right of association, the promotion of political ideas and programs of political action, and the right to vote."[14]

To some extent, the view expressed by Douglas in *Williams v. Rhodes* represented movement from the view he expressed in *Harper v. Virginia Board of Elections*, where, on one reading, he treated the right to vote only as a trigger of strict scrutiny for equal protection. He ended his opinion in *Harper* on this note: "Wealth or fee-paying has in our view no relation to voting qualifications. The right to vote is too precious, too fundamental, to be so burdened or conditioned." In the early section of his opinion in *Harper*, however, Douglas flirted with the idea of grounding the right to vote for state officials, viewed as a direct, independent basis for invalidating the poll tax, on the First Amendment guarantee of free speech. In the end, however, he turned to equal protection, and claimed that it was therefore unnecessary to rule on the issue. Two years later, in his opinion in *Williams v. Rhodes*, Douglas mentioned the Equal Protection Clause, but reduced it to a ban on "invidious discrimination." In *Williams v. Rhodes*, he rested his judgment entirely on the First Amendment (though made applicable to the states by the Fourteenth Amendment), and in so doing he identified the First Amendment and the guarantee of free speech as the source of the right to vote. Although no other justice joined Douglas's concurring opinion in *Williams v. Rhodes* linking the right to vote to the First Amendment, I believe the lack of support might well have been due to the peculiar origins, rather than the merits, of his opinion.[15]

In *Williams v. Rhodes*, Chief Justice Warren took the position that the Court's review of the Ohio electoral scheme and its exclusion of the American Independent Party from the ballot was precipitous. He objected to the Court's decision to accelerate its consideration of the merits and dissented. As a result, Justice Black became the senior justice in the majority, giving him the prerogative to assign the responsibility for writing the opinion for the Court, which he apparently assigned to himself. On October 8, however, the day after argument and conference, Justice Douglas circulated an opinion that purported to be the opinion of the Court. A note explained: "I have taken the liberty of circulating this rough draft opinion with the thought that it might possibly be helpful in expediting our disposition of the cases." On the very next day, that is, October 9, Black circulated his own draft of the Court opinion. Yet on October 10 and 11, Douglas made further revisions on his draft and circulated it to the other justices, which must have compounded the resentment that

Justice Black surely felt by Douglas's rather transparent attempt to claim for himself the privilege of writing the opinion for the Court.

Once it became clear, however, that Black was able to garner the support of Brennan, Marshall, and even Fortas (who had rather strained relations with Black), Douglas changed his draft opinion to make it appear as a concurring opinion rather than as an opinion for the Court. "We" was changed to "I," "It is so ordered" was changed to "Hence I concur in today's decision." Regardless of what they might have thought of the merits, no other justice publicly commented on Douglas's concurring opinion, much less dared to join it. Any other course might well have been read as approving Douglas's transgression of an internal rule of the Court and would have added to the offense that Justice Black must have felt from that transgression—these are proud men.

CONSOLIDATION AND REFORMULATION: FROM THE FOURTEENTH TO THE FIRST AMENDMENT

Justice Black spoke for the Court in *Williams v. Rhodes* and grounded the right of feasible access to the ballot on the Equal Protection Clause of the Fourteenth Amendment. He relied on the fundamental rights branch of strict scrutiny and set aside the Ohio electoral laws for burdening without adequate justification two "precious freedoms," the right to political association and the right to cast an effective vote. Justice Douglas tried to ground the right to feasible access in a different way. He spoke of freedom of association and the right to vote, yet they were not triggers of strict scrutiny and unrelated to equal protection. These freedoms were viewed as constitutional rights and, as such, were direct, independent constraints on the exercise of state power. As a purely formal matter, these constraints were made applicable to the states by the Fourteenth

Amendment (specifically by the Due Process Clause) but were viewed by Douglas as acquiring their status as constitutional rights from the First Amendment guarantee of free speech.

In 1983, fifteen years after *Williams v. Rhodes*, the Court once again gave force to the right of feasible access, but it repudiated the doctrinal framework that Black had created and moved the law closer to the view that Douglas had dared—perhaps too aggressively—to propose. In the 1983 decision in *Anderson v. Celebrezze*, the Supreme Court set aside a newly enacted electoral law of Ohio on the ground that it unduly constrained the choices of voters, and the Court rested its decision entirely on the First Amendment.[16]

With a poetic touch, the Court's opinion in *Anderson v. Celebrezze* was written by John Paul Stevens, who had been appointed by President Gerald Ford in 1975 to fill the vacancy created by Douglas's retirement. Like Douglas, Stevens abandoned the Equal Protection Clause and with it the strict scrutiny test that had been used in *Williams v. Rhodes* to guide the application of that provision. Stevens grounded the rule requiring feasible access in the First Amendment, as a way of protecting the choices of voters, and treated the First Amendment not as a trigger but as a direct, independent right to be protected. However, unlike Douglas, Stevens used a complex balancing test to protect that right and, even more significantly, Stevens saw the First Amendment only as a source of the freedom of association, not as a source of a right to vote. In fact, as in *Crawford v. Marion County Election Board*, the photo ID case discussed in Chapter 3, Stevens abstained from any mention of the right to vote. He did not characterize the right to vote as a constitutional right or even suggest that it was a precious or fundamental right.

Although the Court handed down its ruling in *Anderson v. Celebrezze* in April 1983, the case arose from the presidential election of 1980 in which Ronald Reagan, a Republican, defeated the Democratic incumbent, Jimmy Carter. John Anderson, a longtime

Republican senator representing the liberal wing of the party, formally announced his candidacy for the presidency on June 8, 1979. It was not, however, until April 24, 1980, once he concluded that there was little chance of gaining the Republican nomination, that Anderson announced that he would run as an independent candidate.

At the time of *Williams v. Rhodes*, Ohio did not permit independent candidates. Governor Wallace had challenged the hegemony of the Democratic and Republican parties by presenting himself not as an independent candidate but as the standard-bearer of a new party. Following the Court's decision on Wallace's candidacy, however, Ohio amended its electoral laws to permit independent candidates, provided that they filed formal nominating papers demonstrating significant support by March 20 of the election year. The nominating papers of Anderson contained the requisite number of supporting voter signatures (14,500) but were rejected because they were not submitted to the Ohio secretary of state prior to the March 20 deadline.

A federal district court held the early deadline unconstitutional and, much as the Supreme Court had decreed in *Williams v. Rhodes*, placed Anderson's name on the ballot. Efforts to have that order stayed or set aside by higher federal courts prior to the elections were unsuccessful. The 1980 election went forward with Anderson listed on the Ohio ballot as an independent. He received 5.9% of the Ohio vote and about the same nationally. Ronald Reagan easily won this election. Although the 1980 presidential election had long passed, the Supreme Court, with an eye to establishing the ground rules for future elections, decided that the case was not moot and went on to examine the validity of the early deadline for independents. Especially mindful of the fact that the established parties did not hold their conventions until the late summer, the Court invalidated the law requiring independents to file by March 20.

As with *Williams v. Rhodes*, the primary concern of the Court in *Anderson v. Celebrezze* was the impact of the early deadline, not on the candidate, but on the rights of the electorate. Yet in an early footnote, Stevens created a measure of distance from Black's opinion in *William v. Rhodes* when he declared, "we base our conclusions directly on the First and Fourteenth Amendments and do not engage in a separate Equal Protection Clause analysis."[17] Stevens backtracked somewhat, perhaps to secure the support of Brennan and Marshall, both of whom joined Black's opinion in *Williams v. Rhodes*, when he qualified his avoidance of equal protection by adding, "we rely, however, on the analysis in a number of our prior election cases" that apply "the 'fundamental rights' strand of equal protection analysis." Stevens also made it clear that *Williams v. Rhodes* was one of "our prior election cases" to which he was referring.

As we saw, in *Williams v. Rhodes* Black had identified two fundamental rights—the right of political association and the right to cast a vote effectively—that the Ohio electoral scheme burdened and thus were viewed as triggers for the strict scrutiny test of equal protection. Stevens, in contrast, dropped any reference to the right to vote, or any of its variants, and focused exclusively on the right of political association. Even more importantly, the burden on the right of association was not treated as a trigger for strict scrutiny. Rather, it was the constitutional right that the Court's intervention was designed to protect. Although the strict scrutiny test in *Williams v. Rhodes* was used as a heuristic to guide the application of equal protection, and although in some instances strict scrutiny is used to protect against infringements of First Amendment rights—the source of the right of political association—Stevens went out of his way to make it clear that this right of political association in ballot access cases would not be protected by a strict scrutiny test.

In *Anderson v. Celebrezze*, Stevens specifically disavowed any "litmus-paper test"[18] that would separate invalid from valid restrictions when a court seeks to protect access to the ballot. As opposed to strict scrutiny, he instead relied on a more measured balancing test, referred to as a sliding scale balancing test—the greater the injury, the greater the burden on the state to justify the law causing the injury. As we saw in Chapter 3, when Stevens (and Souter) applied that test to judge state laws governing the administration or management of elections, the sliding scale balancing test requires the Court to consider the character and magnitude of the injury to the right of association, the strength of the interest served by the contested law, and the need to burden the right to serve that interest. "Only after weighing all these factors," Stevens concluded in *Anderson v. Celebrezze*, "is the reviewing court in a position to decide whether the challenged provision is unconstitutional."[19]

In adopting the sliding scale balancing test and thus repudiating strict scrutiny, Stevens not only distanced himself from Black's approach in *Williams v. Rhodes*, he also put himself at odds with Douglas, who found balancing of any type anathema. As Douglas said in *Williams v. Rhodes*, "It is unnecessary to decide whether Ohio has an interest, 'compelling' or not, in abridging those rights, because 'the men who drafted our Bill of Rights did all the "balancing" that was to be done in the field.'"[20] Stevens's opinion in *Anderson v. Celebrezze* departed from Douglas's opinion in *Williams v. Rhodes* in a second and perhaps more important respect. Although both Douglas and Stevens embraced the First Amendment, Douglas saw that amendment as giving rise to a right to vote while Stevens invoked the First Amendment only as the source of the freedom of association. For Stevens, the March filing requirement for independent candidates limits "the opportunities of independent-minded voters to associate in the electoral arena to enhance their political effectiveness as a group."[21]

Stevens's focus on freedom of association pursues a theme that Black introduced in *Williams v. Rhodes* (to lay the groundwork for his application of strict scrutiny and equal protection). Yet, as I said in my analysis of *Williams v. Rhodes*, it is hard to see how the Ohio early filing requirement would interfere with the freedom of association or advocacy for anyone, including independent-minded voters. There is no threat of harassment or retaliation. It only requires independent candidates to file early or, on Stevens's account, too early, to secure a place on the ballot. That may discourage independents from ever declaring their candidacy, but that effect does not constitute a violation of the freedom of association that *NAACP v. Button* sought to protect.

Stevens complained of the limits placed on the opportunity of "independent-minded" persons "to associate in the electoral arena to enhance their political effectiveness as a group." This complaint strikes me as a convoluted way of saying the early deadline prevented Anderson's supporters from voting for him. As such it is a complaint about the interference with the right to vote, not with the freedom of political association. Of course Stevens might be using the right of association as a diplomatic proxy for the right to vote. But even if that is so, his conception of the wrong is distorted. The early filing date in effect limited the opportunity of all the voters of Ohio, not just those who are "independent-minded."

In his lonely concurrence in *Williams v. Rhodes*, Justice Douglas, like Stevens and his majority in *Anderson v. Celebrezze*, pointed to the First Amendment as the source of the requirement of feasible access. Douglas spoke of freedom of association but went beyond Stevens and also complained of the exclusionary effect of the laws governing the ballot on the right to vote. Douglas did not elaborate on that claim. Conceivably, he might have seen the state law as an interference with the right to cast a meaningful vote where meaningfulness is gauged by the understanding that the purpose of an election is to allow those who are ruled to choose their rulers freely. Yet the context in which he spoke of the right to vote—immediately after referring to the "promotion of political ideas and programs of political action"—arguably indicates that he had something similar in mind.[22] Douglas's attempt in *Williams v. Rhodes*, however, to ground on the First Amendment the right to vote or the right to cast a meaningful vote seems misconceived.

Admittedly, the First Amendment's protection of robust public debate may well be intended to enhance collective self-determination —to give voters the ideas and information they need for wisely exercising the franchise.[23] Still, to use that understanding of the purposes for protecting freedom of speech as the basis for implying the right to vote or, better yet, the right to cast a meaningful vote would be a case of the tail wagging the dog. We can safely acknowledge that the protection of free speech implies the existence of the right to vote, and, at the same time, we can go on and insist that the very existence of that right is derived not from the protection of freedom of speech but rather from the democratic character of the Constitution taken as a whole.

Such a view does not ignore or even minimize the guarantee of free speech, but only takes it as one element in a larger and more heterogeneous constellation of features of the Constitution that reveal and affirm its democratic character—the process of ratification, the provisions requiring the election of the members of the House of Representatives and the Senate, the evolved understanding of the Electoral College that makes electors nothing more than the agents of the popular vote, the duty of the United States to guarantee to the states a republican form of government, and the amendments that specifically extend the franchise (the Fourteenth, Fifteenth, Nineteenth, Twenty-Fourth, and Twenty-Sixth Amendments). Such a reading of the Constitution is no more adventuresome, yet entirely more persuasive and satisfying, than one that reads the First Amendment protection of freedom of speech as giving rise to the right to vote.

KENNEDY TO THE RESCUE: THE RIGHT TO CAST A
MEANINGFUL VOTE

Both *Williams v. Rhodes* (1968) and *Anderson v. Celebrezze* (1983) confronted the dangers posed to the right to vote by the constraints of state rules governing access to the ballot. In 1992, in *Burdick v. Takushi*, the Supreme Court once again confronted the dangers posed to political freedom by state laws governing the ballot.[24] In this case, however, the issue arose not from an independent candidate or new party trying to gain access to the ballot, but rather by a state law that prohibited voters from bypassing the ballot altogether and writing in the name of the person the voters wished to hold public office. In contrast to *Williams v. Rhodes* and *Anderson v. Celebrezze*, a majority of the Court upheld the contested state law in *Burdick*. The decision provoked a dissent—this time by Anthony Kennedy—that extended the search for an appropriate constitutional basis for the demand for feasible access.

Following the *Anderson v. Celebrezze* decision in 1983, there were a number of personnel changes that had the effect of lessening the judicial vigilance over the constraints of the ballot that had animated that decision. Rehnquist was elevated to the Chief Justiceship while Antonin Scalia, Clarence Thomas, and David Souter were appointed to the Court. These four helped form the majority in *Burdick v. Takushi*. Rehnquist dissented in *Anderson v. Celebrezze*, as did two other justices—Sandra Day O'Connor and Byron White—who remained on the Court and joined the majority in *Burdick v. Takushi*. Rehnquist, now the chief justice, assigned the task of writing the majority opinion to White, who had dissented in *Williams v. Rhodes* and joined Rehnquist's dissent in *Anderson v. Celebrezze*.[25] In both these cases, White revealed a lack of concern with the Ohio electoral restrictions that had the effect of fencing out independents or third parties—two are enough.

Not all the personnel changes that occurred during the decade between *Anderson v. Celebrezze* and *Burdick v. Takushi* worked in the same direction. One of the new appointees was Anthony Kennedy, who, as I noted, wrote the dissent in *Burdick v. Takushi* and in so doing gave expression to the same outlook that infused the majorities in *Anderson v. Celebrezze* and, before that, *Williams v. Rhodes*—a concern for the ways state legislative control over the ballot might impair the freedom that democracy promises. Kennedy had replaced Lewis Powell, who had dissented in *Anderson v. Celebrezze*. Kennedy's dissent in *Burdick v. Takushi* gained the support of Blackmun and even of Stevens.

To his great credit, Kennedy formulated the right at issue in ballot access cases in a way that avoided the pitfall of Stevens's reference to the associational freedom of independent-minded voters in *Anderson v. Celebrezze* and also of Black's reference to the "right to cast an effective vote" in *Williams v. Rhodes*. "The right at stake here," Kennedy said, "is the right to cast a meaningful vote for the candidate of one's choice."[26] This seems a great advance over the formulation of Black (the right to cast a vote effectively) or Douglas (the right to vote). Yet we are left to wonder what might be the source for this right to cast a meaningful vote. Kennedy spoke in only the most glancing fashion about the First and Fourteenth Amendments, without any sustained effort to locate the source of this right in some particular provision of the Constitution. The reader might even have reason to believe that Kennedy is interpreting the Constitution as a whole.

The technical issue before the Court in *Burdick v. Takushi* was the legality of Hawaii's electoral scheme that, in effect, banned write-in votes in both primary and general elections. Among the many arguments advanced on behalf of the write-in, the would-be voter claimed, as White put it, "that he is entitled to cast and Hawaii required to count a 'protest vote' for Donald Duck."[27] Wisely, White summarily rejected that argument; and so did Kennedy. Kennedy explained, "[a]s the majority points out, the purpose of casting, counting, and recording votes is to elect public officials, not to serve as a general forum for political expression."[28] Speaking more generally, Kennedy declared that the petitioner's "right to freedom of expression is not implicated,"[29] which suggests to me that Kennedy, if pushed, might well have grounded the right to cast a meaningful vote not on the First Amendment but on the democratic character of the Constitution taken as a whole.

Kennedy did not speak, in so many terms, of the democratic purposes of the Constitution. Yet he couched his objection to the ban on write-ins in terms that reflect a keen awareness of the distinctly democratic character of our Constitution:

> The majority's approval of Hawaii's ban is ironic at a time when the new democracies in foreign countries strive to emerge from an era of sham elections in which the name of the ruling party candidate was the only one on the ballot. Hawaii does not impose as severe a restriction on the right to vote, but it imposes a restriction that has a haunting similarity in its tendency to exact severe penalties for one who does anything but vote the dominant party ballot.[30]

This passage was written in 1992. Anyone reading the references to "new democracies" at that time would have surely remembered the world historic events that Kennedy was referring to—the collapse of the Berlin Wall, the liberation from Soviet control of a number of countries in Central and Eastern Europe that soon followed, and then, in 1991, the dissolution of the Soviet Union itself. These events no doubt deepened his appreciation of the distinctive features of the

American Constitution and the importance of what I call its guiding ideal—democracy.

White began his opinion in *Burdick v. Takushi* defending the ban on write-ins by extolling the easy access Hawaii provided to the ballot. Granted, to obtain a place on the general election ballot, a candidate must participate in a primary, but Hawaii provided three separate mechanisms by which a candidate might do so: either as a candidate for an established party, as a candidate for a new party, or as a candidate in a non-partisan primary. Moreover, advancing from the non-partisan primary to the general election was easy. The candidate had to receive ten of the votes in that primary election or the number of votes sufficient to nominate a partisan candidate, whichever was lower. Similarly, the requirements for forming a new party also appeared easy: fifteen to twenty-five supporting signatures, filed sixty days before that party's primary election.

The flaw in the system, as Kennedy stressed in his dissent, arose from two facts. One was the rule that limited people to vote in only one primary election, which meant that if individuals voted in a non-partisan primary or new party primary, they must forego the opportunity to vote in the primaries of the established parties. The second fact is that the Democratic Party dominated in Hawaii and had done so for a long time. This meant a voter who voted in the primary of a new party or in a non-partisan primary had to forego the opportunity to participate in probably the only primary that counted—that of the Democratic Party. It was this interlocking system that constrained voter choice, reinforced the dominance of the Democratic Party, and accounted for the fact that, for example, in general elections for the state legislature, 33% of the positions were uncontested. A good number of the voters who did not vote in these uncontested races presumably would have voted if they were allowed to skip the partisan or non-partisan primary system and write in the name of a candidate. The openness of the Hawaiian system was, to Kennedy, actually an illusion.

One would have thought that White's way of proceeding would have yielded a rule tailored to the openness of Hawaii's rules governing access to the ballot: the ban on write-ins is lawful whenever access to the ballot is so easy. But, in a move arguably revealing of his larger ambitions and those of the majority, White created a presumption of legality for a ban on write-ins in all electoral systems. According to White, the presumption of legality arises whenever the restrictions on ballot access are deemed reasonable. This general rule, confining voters to the choices provided on the ballot, ignores the role that the availability of write-ins plays in determining whether the system is sufficiently open or reasonable. As Kennedy stressed, it is circular. In addition, the presumption of legality for a ban on write-ins that White created undermines the applicability of the sliding scale balancing test, which White, at least nominally, endorsed in *Burdick v. Takushi*. It assumes the harm to voters created by the ban on write-in voting is slight and relieves the state from identifying the precise interest needed to justify the imposition of such a burden.

In part, Hawaii defended the ban on write-ins in terms familiar to all the ballot access cases: the desire to avoid excessive factionalism, to deny an outlet for sore losers, and to minimize the risk of voter confusion. This defense of the ban on write-ins is characterized by both the generality of the defenses offered by the state and the fact that they had been rejected in *William v. Rhodes* and *Anderson v. Celebrezze*—the two foundational decisions creating the law of ballot access and the constitutional need for feasible ballot access for third parties and independent candidates. Although White dissented in both cases, in his opinion for the Court in *Burdick v. Takushi*, he cited these decisions approvingly, as though precedent mattered. *William v. Rhodes* and *Anderson v. Celebrezze* involved restrictions on access to the ballot, not a ban on write-ins, but the rejected rationales had no greater persuasiveness when transferred to the new context.

The ban on write-ins did involve one new justification offered by the state, specifically the state's interest in making sure that candidates who are not eligible to hold office are not elected. Kennedy fully appreciated that risk, but insisted that the ban on write-ins was broader than need be to achieve that goal. As he explained, Hawaii could, as approximately twenty states do, require that write-in candidates file a few days before the election a declaration of candidacy and verify that they are eligible to hold office.

In a late-added footnote (footnote 10), White accused Kennedy of betraying the assertion Kennedy had made in his dissent that he, like the majority, was applying the sliding scale balancing test announced by Stevens in *Anderson v. Celebrezze*. This charge overlooks the fact that Stevens joined Kennedy's dissent in *Burdick v. Takushi*. In addition, this charge was based on the mistaken assumption that the narrow tailoring requirement employed by Kennedy belongs only to strict scrutiny. Stevens did not use the term narrow tailoring in *Anderson v. Celebrezze*, but he contemplated the same requirement in his original formulation of the sliding scale balancing test. As Stevens then said, "In passing judgment, the Court must not only determine the legitimacy and strength of each of those interests [offered to justify the burden]; it also must consider the extent to which those interests make it necessary to burden the plaintiff's rights."[31] Moreover, in refusing to validate in *Anderson v. Celebrezze* the early filing requirement on the theory that it enhanced the understanding or education of the voters about the candidates and issues, Justice Stevens acknowledged the importance of that interest. He also stressed, in perhaps the most salient paragraph of his opinion, that this interest could be satisfied in ways that did not require independent candidates to file their nominating papers in March.[32]

Speaking more generally, let me say that Stevens was entirely right when he insisted, in both the formulation of his sliding scale balancing test and its application in *Anderson v. Celebrezze*, that any justification of a law that interferes with a constitutionally protected right necessarily includes a consideration of alternatives that might avoid that interference. We should not view the narrow tailoring requirement as an artifact of strict scrutiny. As Justice Souter fully acknowledged in his dissent in *Crawford v. Marion County Election Board*, narrow tailoring is only a specific formulation of a general proposition of constitutional law that requires the state, in furthering its interests, to choose the alternative that minimizes the sacrifice of prized constitutional values such as freedom or equality.

In *Burdick v. Takushi*, the Supreme Court upheld the Hawaii ban on write-ins and then generalized the ruling by creating a presumption of legality for such bans. Put otherwise, the ruling in *Burdick v. Takushi* declares that the state has no *obligation* to establish a scheme for allowing write-in voting. The Court did not, however, deny the states *permission* to allow write-ins. White stated, in a footnote (footnote 11) at the very end of the opinion, "We of course in no way suggest that a State is not free to provide write-in voting, as many states do; nor should this opinion be read to discourage such provisions."[33] The very placement of this note and the fact that it only makes explicit what was abundantly implicit elsewhere in the opinion suggest that White's purpose was to reassure some justice who had been reluctant to join the opinion. In any event, it remains to be seen whether this grant of permission, even if it is taken up by every state in the Union, would lessen the constraints imposed by ballots and hence the capacity of the election to generate political freedom—the power of the ruled to choose their rulers.

The 1968 decision in *Williams v. Rhodes* seemed to indicate a negative answer to that question. It suggested that write-ins are no substitute for feasible access. The federal district court in that case found restrictive election laws unconstitutional and by way of remedy allowed the American Independent Party and the Socialist Labor Party to obtain the advantage of write-ins (not allowed by Ohio at that time). But when the Supreme Court also concluded that the Ohio electoral scheme was unconstitutional, it set aside the write-in remedy imposed by the district court, ordering that the ballots be revised and the American Independent Party's candidate be allowed to appear on the ballot. As Douglas explained in his opinion in *Williams v. Rhodes* justifying this remedy, "write-ins are no substitute for a place on the ballot."[34] The appearance of the party on the ballot would give greater visibility to the candidates and require less of the voter.

Douglas's view was amplified in *Anderson v. Celebrezze* when Stevens sought to account for the change in Ohio election laws that in the 1980s allowed write-ins. In that case, Stevens wrote: "It is true, of course, that Ohio permits 'write-in' votes for independents. We have previously noted that this opportunity is not an adequate substitute for having the candidate's name appear on the printed ballot."[35] Stevens then went on to quote from the Court's opinion in *Lubin v. Panish*, which explained the disadvantages entailed in write-ins not just to the candidate but also to the voter.[36] A candidate, the Court explained in *Lubin v. Panish*, "relegated to the write-in provision, would be forced to rest his chances solely on those voters who remember his name and take the affirmative step of writing it on the ballot."[37] In the 1980 election, 5.7 million votes were cast for persons appearing on the Ohio ballot. Only 27, Stevens noted, were cast for write-in candidates.

We may therefore safely assume that write-ins are no substitute for a name appearing on the ballot. We must also recognize, however, that in the many decades that have passed since *Williams v. Rhodes* and *Anderson v. Celebrezze* were handed down—one in 1968, the other in 1983—we have experienced, due to the development of digital technology and the advent of the internet and social media, a revolution in the means of communication. This revolution will not close the gap between write-ins and those appearing on the ballot or lessen the importance of the constitutional requirement that state electoral laws provide feasible access for third parties and independents. The write-in remains the less preferred instrument for expanding the choices of voters or enabling voters to cast a meaningful vote. Yet the new technology might render the write-in a more viable democratic option. It might enhance the capacity of those who might be denied a place on the official ballot to obtain greater name recognition or even to raise the funds needed to mount an effective write-in campaign. Remember, the issue is not whether a write-in candidate is likely to win, or even whether write-ins will force the major parties to change or even reexamine their position. The issue is whether the new technology will enhance, as Kennedy might put it, the capacity of voters to cast a meaningful vote. Success is measured not by the results (the votes a candidate garners), but by the freedom that is experienced.

To imagine such democratic possibilities in face of the decision in *Burdick v. Takushi* presumes that all or most of the states will take advantage of the permission the Court extended in footnote 11. Even more, it presumes that we remain true to our resolve to preserve the protection of freedom of speech—not as the source of the right to vote, nor as the source of the right to cast a meaningful vote, nor even as the source of the freedom of political association, but rather as the background condition that makes any form of voting meaningful.

Conclusion

...

Is the Law of Democracy Really Law?

IN 1998, THREE then-young scholars—Samuel Issacharoff, Pamela Karlan, and Richard Pildes—published a book titled *The Law of Democracy*. The book was intended for use in law school classes and the publisher, Foundation Press, included the book in its University Casebook Series.

Like all the books in Foundation's series, *The Law of Democracy* built upon the governing statutes, constitutional provisions, and the most important law review articles and books. For the most part, however, the book consisted of a collection of judicial opinions, primarily those rendered by the Supreme Court when it was called upon to give concrete meaning and expression to the broad and general provisions of the Constitution. It was these opinions of the Supreme Court that constituted, so it seemed to me, the law of democracy and that was to be the principal subject of study and discussion in the classroom.

Why We Vote. Owen Fiss, Oxford University Press. © Owen Fiss 2024.
DOI: 10.1093/oso/9780197746387.003.0007

The book has been enormously successful. Over the last twenty-five years, it has gone through several editions, has grown considerably in length, and the authors have conscientiously kept abreast of the new rulings of the Supreme Court. Even more significantly, the book has begun to shape the standard law school curriculum, sparking the emergence of new courses devoted to the law of democracy. A number of senior professors—I was one—adjusted their familiar offerings to create the room that would enable them to teach a course defined by *The Law of Democracy*. In time, some of the brightest lights in the new generation of law teachers became specialists in the subject and built careers out of this book. In this way, *The Law of Democracy* managed to create, as the authors had originally hoped, a new field of study. As such, it stands as a tribute to the authors' knowledge and imagination, as well as to their pedagogical instincts.

I taught the book on a number of occasions. After the second or third time, I ended the course with a doubt that I eventually summoned the courage to express: Is the law of democracy really law? This was not a doubt about the quality of the book, but rather about the judicial opinions that the authors collected and presented in their book. Do these decisions, taken in their entirety, constitute what might properly be called the law of democracy? Were the decisions really law? Of course, the answer to that question in part turns on another—what is law?—that has long bedeviled legal scholars.

In the early nineteenth century, a distinguished English philosopher, John Austin, famously answered this question by defining law as the commands of the sovereign backed by force. Later in the century, Oliver Wendell Holmes, then a justice of the Supreme Judicial Court of Massachusetts but soon to become a justice of the Supreme Court of the United States, enlarged this perspective in a lecture to students that he eventually published in the Harvard Law Review.

In "The Path of the Law," Holmes sought to distinguish law from morality and did so by emphasizing the perspective of the bad man and the fears that he might harbor, specifically that violations of law will be met by the force of the state. For Holmes, like Austin, law binds in a way that morality does not, and the binding quality of the law arises from and justifies the fact that the state is prepared to use its power to enforce or implement its requirements.

I have no doubt that the many pronouncements of the Supreme Court that have been collected and presented in *The Law of Democracy* are binding on the nation. The power of the federal government can and, whenever necessary, should be used to enforce the edicts of the Supreme Court. The doubt that I had expressed at the end of class about the Supreme Court rulings was not, however, addressed to their binding character. Rather, it stemmed from a recognition of the terms and conditions that limit the Court's capacity to make law. The Supreme Court is not a "sovereign" with the capacity or even the inclination to issue what John Austin referred to as "commands."

The Supreme Court's law-making power is limited. It arises from the authority of the Supreme Court to interpret the Constitution and, like any court, the Supreme Court is required to give reasons for these interpretations. Admittedly, the decisions collected and presented in *The Law of Democracy* offer reasons to justify the rulings and the specific rules that the Court promulgates. Yet, for the most part, those reasons have little to do with democracy. These opinions of the Supreme Court do not rest on a clear and crisp understanding of democracy nor do the rulings of the Court rest on a comprehensive, autonomous body of principles that might give specific content to the democratic purpose of the Constitution. That this failure to justify decisions impairs the persuasiveness of the opinions is no small blemish. It not only impairs the persuasiveness of the opinions but also undermines the very capacity of the Court to generate the admiration that rightly belongs to law, an admiration that, as a general matter, provides the reason for us to obey the law.

The cases presented to the Court deal with the familiar practices and institutions associated in the popular mind with democracy: elections, voting, electoral districts, political parties, ballots. The opinions of the Supreme Court formulate the rules that will govern these practices and institutions. How the Court decides these cases shapes our democratic practices and institutions, but only as a consequence. For the most part, the specific rules that the Court has propounded have not been derived from any clear understanding of democracy or the purposes it serves, or the reasons we value it. Instead, they have been derived from the application of constitutional provisions, such as equal protection or freedom of speech, which of course serve worthy purposes, though those purposes differ in significant ways and are thus sometimes orthogonal to those served by democracy.

As a result, the vast collection of Supreme Court decisions presented in *The Law of Democracy* do not leave, in the mind of either the teacher or the students, a comprehensive understanding of the purposes of democracy nor of its requirements. Instead of a law of democracy, these decisions might be read as yielding a law governing elections or voting. Alternatively, they may be understood as constituting a special branch of equal protection or free speech doctrine. Either way, they fall short of producing a law of democracy, even though vague, loosely, and fleetingly espoused sentiments about democracy may have sometimes guided the interpretation of these provisions, at least as they apply to elections or voting. In speaking of *The Law of Democracy*, we are reminded of the famous treatises of the common law, such as *The Law of Contracts*, but the legal doctrine that emerges from this compendium is entirely more fragmentary or partial than is suggested by its sweeping title.

Even more significantly, the doctrine that might be extracted from these cases is less admirable or worthy than it would be if it rested on the reasoned elaboration of democracy as a constitutional value. Trying to justify rules that the Court announces on the basis of the Equal Protection Clause is strained or artificial, for that provision says nothing more than the state shall not "deny any person within its jurisdiction the equal protection of the laws." The same could be said about the effort to justify, on the basis of the free speech guarantee of the First Amendment, a rule protecting, as the ballot access cases such as *Williams v. Rhodes* and *Anderson v. Celebrezzi* do, the right to cast a meaningful vote or to vote effectively. That provision only commands that "Congress shall make no law . . . abridging the freedom of speech."

Sometimes the justices seem to get closer to the mark when they, in *Reynolds v. Sims*, for example, or *Harper v. Virginia Board of Elections*, characterize the right to vote as "precious" or "fundamental" and do so on the basis of the role of the right to vote in a democratic system of government. Yet they lose their way when they treat violations of the right to vote only as a trigger of strict scrutiny—a heuristic that merely requires the state, in defending itself from a charge that it is denying equal protection or abridging the freedom of speech, to prove that the contested law is necessary to achieve a compelling public purpose. They fail to treat the right to vote as an independent, substantive right, one that stands apart from the right to equal protection or freedom of speech, but is rather derived from the democratic aspirations of the Constitution.

The cause of this sorry state of affairs is clear. It derives from two facts. One is the transformation in recent years of the process of constitutional interpretation into one of clause-parsing and the second is that, despite the fact that there are countless provisions that reveal its democratic purposes, there is no clause in the Constitution that, in so many terms, guarantees democracy. Although clause-parsing may have some virtues—it highlights and emphasizes the written character of the Constitution—it distorts the interpretive endeavor by treating the Constitution as though it were a contract. It blinds the Court to the whole and the purposes that the whole serves. In a professional setting dominated by the practice of clause-parsing, a justice charged with writing the opinion of the Court feels compelled to hunt for and hopefully locate a clause or maybe two that can serve as the source or basis of the ruling. Such a search belittles the overarching democratic purposes of the Constitution and makes it difficult to acknowledge or honor democracy as a guiding or regulatory ideal of the Constitution.

Sometimes, these professional norms even lead a justice to construct out of a word or two appearing in the Constitution an entirely new clause. This occurred in *Wesberry v. Sanders* when Justice Black pounced on the phrase "by the People" in Article I to justify a rule requiring equal number of voters in each congressional district. It also occurred in Rehnquist's concurrence in *Bush v. Gore*, which has evolved into something referred to as the Independent Legislature Doctrine (almost a clause). Rehnquist focused on the word "legislature" appearing in Article II to give the Supreme Court of the United States the power to set aside, as a violation of the federal Constitution, a decision of the Florida Supreme Court that sought to interpret the Florida constitutional provisions regarding elections.

The remedy for this self-induced blindness lies at hand: look at the whole.[1] View the Constitution not as a contract but as the charter of the nation. Start a new tradition that acknowledges the democratic purposes of the Constitution and then formulate doctrine that will give specific content to democracy as a guiding ideal of the Constitution.

Although such an interpretive strategy departs from the norms that governed the many decisions presented in *The Law of Democracy*, it can find refuge and support in another branch of the law—separation of powers.[2] There is no clause guaranteeing the separation of powers, though, of course, the Constitution sets out the powers and duties of each branch of the federal government in separate articles (Articles I, II, and III). The Supreme Court has viewed the separation of powers principle as a guiding ideal of the Constitution and used it to set aside the actions of the President or Congress that exceed the bounds of one branch's powers and usurps those of another.

The separation of powers principle received its most emphatic endorsement in *Youngstown Sheet & Tube Co. v. Sawyer* (1952), in which the Supreme Court set aside President Harry S. Truman's seizure of the steel industry in order to ensure the continued production of steel during the Korean War. Justice Black wrote the opinion for the Court, and his opinion is reminiscent of the opinion that he was to write later, in 1964, for the Court in *Wesberry v. Sanders*. In *Youngstown*, Black sought to justify the Court's decision to set aside Truman's action on the words of the Constitution (less than a clause) that gave Congress the power "to make law." This defense of the Court's decision proved utterly unconvincing and has been eclipsed by the concurring opinion filed in that case by Justice Robert Jackson.

In this concurrence, Jackson gave content to the separation of powers principle through the process of reasoned elaboration, insisting that "[t]he actual art of governing under our Constitution does not and cannot conform to judicial definitions of the power of any of its branches based on isolated clauses or even single Articles torn from context." Approaching the task in front of him from this perspective, Jackson identified the overarching purposes of separation of powers—"[t]he purpose of the Constitution was not only to grant power, but to keep it from getting out of hand"—and then proceeded to develop a doctrine that would serve those purposes and constitute the framework for "a workable government." Jackson's opinion, in contrast to the one filed by Black in *Youngstown*, has long been admired and respected by the legal profession and is viewed as the one that more fully satisfies the higher purposes of the law.

This book treats Jackson's *Youngstown* opinion and his method of transcending the strictures of clause-bound constitutional interpretation as exemplary. The subject is not separation of powers but rather democracy. It treats democracy as a first principle and extends an invitation to some especially courageous justice or a group of justices, or maybe an entire new generation of lawyers, to transcend the limits imposed on them by the now dominant practice of clause-parsing. It urges them to look at the whole. This invitation is founded on the idea that democracy is the source of our political freedom and calls for the formulation of judicial doctrine that protects and nourishes that freedom.

At the heart of such an endeavor would be a full and uncompromising recognition of the right to vote, not as an appendage to equal protection or associational freedom, nor even as a fundamental right, but rather as a constitutional right of its own, with all the promise and limitations fitting that status. The right to vote is the means by which the ruled participate in the process of selecting their rulers and thus is essential for the fulfillment of the democratic purpose of the Constitution. It presumes that one person's right to vote is as worthy as another's.

I also maintain that, in the name of enhancing the domain of political freedom, the right to vote should be governed by two subsidiary principles: the requirement of coextensionality and the duty of facilitation. The first seeks to extend the franchise to all who are ruled and the second imposes an affirmative duty on the states to manage the election process in a way that minimizes the practical difficulties citizens might experience in trying to exercise the right to vote. The purpose of an election, as Congress once recognized, is not to exhaust the voter but to ascertain the will of the majority.

The capacity of an election to do just that demands, in addition, that we relax the constraints imposed by the official ballot on the choices available to voters. In order to render the right to vote meaningful, the judiciary must make certain that independent candidates and new parties have a good and fair chance to get on the ballot. They are entitled to feasible access.

In all these ways, the judiciary will, through the familiar process of reasoned elaboration, develop doctrine that gives specific content to the right to vote, much like it does with every federal constitutional right. In this instance, the judiciary will be acting for a near transcendent and now especially urgent purpose—to honor the democratic aspirations of the Constitution.

Acknowledgments

. . .

The idea for this book first took shape in a seminar that I taught in the spring of 2020, as the COVID-19 pandemic spread and eventually brought to an abrupt end our capacity to meet in person. I am grateful to the students in that seminar for their spirited comments and reflections. One of them, Cara Meyer, played a pivotal role in the class discussions and later, for the next two years, served as my editor and research assistant. This book bears the mark of her intelligence, good judgment, endless curiosity, and abundant literary skills.

I am also grateful to Lydia Fuller, Sarah Walker, Jordan Jefferson, Alaa Hachem, and Adam Flaherty for their research and editorial assistance. The manuscript was prepared during the most difficult of circumstances, the COVID-19 lockdown, and the credit for that remarkable feat belongs to Bradley Hayes.

I owe a special debt of gratitude to Geoffrey Stone, the editor of the series in which this book appears and a professor at the University of Chicago. He warmly embraced this project when the manuscript was first presented to him and urged revisions that greatly improved it.

Notes

...

INTRODUCTION

1. ALEXANDER MEIKLEJOHN, Free Speech and Its Relation to Self-Government (1948), *in* POLITICAL FREEDOM: THE CONSTITUTIONAL POWERS OF THE PEOPLE 3 (1960).

CHAPTER 1

1. Reva B. Siegel, *She the People: The Nineteenth Amendment, Sex Equality, Federalism, and the Family*, 115 HARV. L. REV. 948 (2002).

2. Chiafalo v. Washington, 140 S. Ct. 2316 (2020).

3. *Id.* at 2328.

4. *Id.*

5. In *Colorado Department of State v. Baca* (2020), three of Colorado's electors from the 2016 election sued the Colorado Department of State, alleging that the Colorado law requiring presidential electors to vote for the candidate chosen by the popular vote was unconstitutional. Mr. Baca voted for John Kasich, despite the state's popular vote for Hillary Clinton, and the Colorado Secretary of State discarded his vote and removed him as an elector. After briefing and arguments, the Court issued a brief per curiam

opinion upholding Colorado's law for the reasons stated by Justice Kagan in *Chiafalo v. Washington*.

6. Texas v. Pennsylvania, 141 S. Ct. 1230 (Dec. 11, 2020). In addition, on February 22, 2021, the Supreme Court declined to issue a writ of certiorari in a case challenging, on federal constitutional grounds, a decision of the Supreme Court of Pennsylvania that had construed Pennsylvania's electoral laws to allow extending the time for the receipt of mail-in ballots in order to accommodate COVID-19 postal delays. Republican Party of Pennsylvania v. Degraffenreid, 141 S. Ct. 732 (2021). This challenge had first been presented to the Court immediately before the election and renewed soon thereafter, but the Court refused to issue a stay of the order of the Supreme Court of Pennsylvania.

7. 347 U.S. 483, 495 (1954).

8. *See, e.g.*, Louisiana v. United States, 380 U.S. 145 (1965); United States v. Mississippi, 380 U.S. 128 (1965).

9. *See generally* Brian Landsberg, Free at Last to Vote: The Alabama Origins of the 1965 Voting Rights Act (2007).

10. 383 U.S. 301 (1966).

11. 377 U.S. 533 (1964).

12. 383 U.S. 663 (1966).

13. Wesberry v. Sanders, 376 U.S. 1 (1964).

14. 376 U.S. 254 (1964).

15. 372 U.S. 335 (1963).

16. Ronald Dworkin, *The Forum of Principle*, 56 N.Y.U. L. Rev. 469 (1981).

17. 377 U.S. at 560 (quoting *Wesberry*, 376 U.S. at 17).

18. 383 U.S. at 670.

19. 369 U.S. 186, 242 (1962) (Douglas, J., concurring).

20. 2 U.S. 419, 457 (1793) (Wilson, J., concurring).

21. 347 U.S. 497 (1954).

22. *Id.* at 500.

23. 377 U.S. at 554.

24. 383 U.S. at 665.

25. *Id.*

26. *Id.* at 665 n.2 (quoting United States v. Texas, 252 F. Supp. 234, 254 (W.D. Tex. 1966)).

CHAPTER 2

1. Gaston County v. United States, 395 U.S. 285 (1969); *see also* Owen Fiss, *Gaston County v. United States: Fruition of the Freezing Principle*, 1969 SUP. CT. REV. 379.

2. 570 U.S. 529 (2013).

3. Korematsu v. United States, 323 U.S. 214, 216 (1944).

4. Williams v. Rhodes, 393 U.S. 23, 39 (1968) (Douglas, J., concurring).

5. In the year before *Harper*, the Court, in *Carrington v. Rash*, 380 U.S. 89 (1965), invalidated Texas's ban on voting for members of the military who had moved into the state. In prohibiting military members from voting, Texas purportedly sought to prevent the "takeover" of community interests by a short-term population. Justice Potter Stewart, writing for the majority, held that while Texas may institute a residency requirement on the right to vote, it must give military members the opportunity to show that they are bona fide residents. Relying on the Equal Protection Clause, Stewart described Texas's voting ban as a violation because it was "fencing out" a sector of the population. Although Stewart rejected the state's complete ban as unnecessary for the residency interests it sought to protect, he did not formally apply the fundamental rights branch of strict scrutiny and in fact, subsequently, in a strongly worded dissent, objected to Warren's application of that test in *Kramer v. Union Free School District No. 15*, 395 U.S. 621, 634 (1969).

6. 395 U.S. 621 (1969).

7. 405 U.S. 330 (1972).

8. In March 1973, Justice Powell wrote the opinion for a majority of five—Stewart plus the four Nixon appointees—that denied, for purposes of applying the fundamental rights branch of strict scrutiny, that education was a fundamental right. Among a broad variety of arguments, the counsel for the aggrieved parents maintained that even if the right to education were not itself a fundamental right, any limitations on education would adversely affect the exercise of a right—namely the right to vote—that was, under established doctrine, most assuredly a fundamental right. In his dissent, Marshall embraced this argument. Powell was of another mind. He dismissed the counsel's argument by drawing a distinction between the protection of the right to vote and a far more ambitious—indeed too ambitious for Powell—goal of guaranteeing a fully informed electoral choice.

Before reaching that conclusion, however, Powell inserted this remark about the right to vote in a footnote. He there said: "Since the right to vote, per se, is not a constitutionally protected right, we assume that the appellees' references to that right are simply shorthand references to the protected right, implicit in our constitutional system, to participate in state elections on an equal basis with other qualified voters whenever the State has adopted an elective process for determining who will represent any segment of the States' population." San Antonio Indep. School Dist. v. Rodriguez, 411 U.S. 1, 35 n.78 (1973).

9. 418 U.S. 24 (1974).

10. *See* note 25 in Chapter 5.

11. Owen Fiss & Charles Krauthammer, *The Rehnquist Court*, THE NEW REPUBLIC (Mar. 10, 1982).

12. 418 U.S. at 79 (Marshall, J., dissenting).

13. *Id.* at 81 (Marshall, J., dissenting).

14. *Id.* at 82–83 (Marshall, J., dissenting).

15. *Id.* at 82 (Marshall, J., dissenting).

16. 471 U.S. 222 (1985).

17. 426 U.S. 229 (1976).

18. 429 U.S. 252 (1977).

19. 471 U.S. at 232 ("[I]t is beyond peradventure that [the purpose to discriminate against all blacks] was a 'but-for' motivation for the enactment of § 182.").

20. *Id.*

21. *Id.* at 233.

22. *Id.*

23. Katzenbach v. Morgan, 384 U.S. 641 (1966).

24. City of Boerne v. Flores, 521 U.S. 507 (1997).

25. *See, e.g.*, Bouie v. City of Columbia, 378 U.S. 347 (1964).

26. Jones v. DeSantis, 410 F. Supp. 3d 1284 (N.D. Fla. 2019).

27. Jones v. Governor of Florida, 950 F.3d 795 (11th Cir. 2020).

28. Jones v. DeSantis, 462 F. Supp. 3d 1196 (N.D. Fla. 2020).

29. Raysor v. DeSantis, 140 S. Ct. 2600 (2020).

30. Stephen Breyer, *Our Democratic Constitution*, 77 N.Y.U. L. REV. 245 (2002).

31. Jones v. Governor of Florida, 975 F.3d 1016 (11th Cir. 2020).

32. Only in dissent did the judges point out the larger significance of voting to our democratic order. *See* Jones v. Governor of Florida, 975 F.3d 1016, 1083 (11th Cir. 2020) (Judge Jordan joined by Judges Wilson, Martin, and Jill Pryor dissenting).

33. As of October 2022, 2.23 million persons over eighteen are denied the right to vote because of their felony convictions, even though they have served their sentences and completed the terms of their parole and probation. This breach of the coextensionality requirement affects about 1% of the voting age population in the United States, though the significance of this number, for the election of federal as well as state officials, is magnified by the fact that the disenfranchisement arises from the laws of only eleven states: Alabama, Arizona, Delaware, Florida, Iowa, Kentucky, Mississippi, Nebraska, Tennessee, Virginia, and Wyoming. *See* Christopher Uggen et al., *Locked Out 2022: Estimates of People Denied Voting Rights Due to a Felony Conviction*, THE SENTENCING PROJECT 4 (Oct. 2022), https://www.sentencingproject.org/app/uploads/2022/10/Locked-Out-2022-Estimates-of-People-Denied-Voting.pdf. More recently, the Governor of Virginia issued an executive order allowing those who are not currently incarcerated to vote. That order was first introduced by the Governor in March 2021 and then continued by his successor in January 2022. *See Criminal Disenfranchisement Laws Across the United States*, BRENNAN CTR. FOR JUST. 5 (Aug. 5, 2022).

34. For a more universalistic and arguably more generous perspective *see* Chapter 10, "Who Are the People?" in Jedediah Purdy, Two Cheers for Politics (2022), p. 208: "Whoever is within a national territory, living with the law of the country, should have the choice of taking political citizenship and a role in shaping or approving those laws."

35. The Virgin Islands, Guam, and Northern Mariana Islands are governed by a similar statute granting United States citizenship to persons born in these territories. The statute governing American Samoa is significantly more constrained, for it declares that persons born in the territory "are nationals but not citizens of the United States." *See Fitisemanu v. United States*, 1 F.4th 862 (10th Cir. 2021), upholding the limitation on citizenship.

CHAPTER 3

1. Article I, Section 4 reads: "The Times, Places and Manner of holding Elections for Senators and Representatives, shall be prescribed in each State by the Legislature thereof; but the Congress may at any time by Law make or alter such Regulations, except as to the Places of chusing Senators."

2. 553 U.S. 181 (2008).

3. 460 U.S. 780 (1983).

4. 504 U.S. 428 (1992).

5. Justice Stevens joined the dissent in *Burdick v. Takushi*, which was written by Justice Kennedy. Kennedy explicitly embraced the sliding scale balancing test in his dissent, but was even more coy than White in identifying the underlying the constitutional right (*see* Chapter 5).

6. 553 U.S. at 190.

7. *Id*. at 210 (Souter, J., dissenting).

8. *Id*. (Souter, J., dissenting).

9. *Id*. at 200.

10. *Id*. at 212–13 (Souter, J., dissenting).

11. *Id*. at 236 (Souter, J., dissenting).

12. *Id*. at 220 (Souter, J., dissenting).

13. Id. at 220 n.24 (Souter, J., dissenting).

14. *Id*. at 202 n.20.

15. *Id*.

16. *See* text at note 20 in Chapter 4, which discusses Souter's dissenting opinion in *Bush v. Gore*. It too recognizes the fundamentality of the right to vote.

17. 553 U.S. at 189.

18. In his concurrence in *Nixon v. Shrink Missouri Government PAC*, 528 U.S. 377, 910 (2000), Justice Breyer first announced his attraction to the proportionality test. Justice Ginsburg joined that concurrence, but not his dissent in *Crawford*.

19. 533 U.S. at 207 (Scalia, J., concurring) (emphasis in original).

20. *Id*.

21. 494 U.S. 872 (1990).

22. 533 U.S. at 208 (Scalia, J., concurring).

23. *Id*.

24. *Id.* at 207n*.

25. This speculation is based on Justice Alito's opinion in *Brnovich v. DNC*, 141 S. Ct. 2321 (2021), which rejected an attack, based on the Voting Rights Act of 1965, on Arizona's election regulations on the theory that the impact of those regulations was not severe.

26. 553 U.S. at 208 (Scalia, J., concurring) The entire sentence reads: "It is for state legislatures to weigh the costs and benefits of possible changes to their election codes, and their judgment must prevail unless it imposes a severe and unjustified overall burden upon the right to vote, or is intended to disadvantage a particular class."

CHAPTER 4

1. Reynolds v. Sims, 377 U.S. 533 at 551 (1964).

2. *Id.* at 562.

3. *Id.* at 562–63.

4. White v. Regester, 412 U.S. 755 (1973).

5. 478 U.S. 30 (1986).

6. 376 U.S. 1 (1964).

7. *Id.* at 20 (Harlan, J., dissenting).

8. *Id.* at 7.

9. 377 U.S. at 561.

10. *Id.* at 559.

11. *Id.* at 574.

12. *Id.*

13. Salyer Land Co. v. Tulare Lake Basin Water Storage Dist., 410 U.S. 719 (1973).

14. *Id.* at 728.

15. Mahan v. Howell, 410 U.S. 315 (1973).

16. *Id.* at 324–25.

17. Bd. of Estimate of City of New York v. Morris, 489 U.S. 688 (1989).

18. *Id.* at 694.

19. 531 U.S. 98 (2000).

20. *Id.* at 134 (Souter, J., dissenting).

21. *Id.* at 103.

22. *Id.* at 110.

23. *Id.* at 109.

24. Bouie v. City of Columbia, 378 U.S. 347 (1964).

25. 531 U.S. at 115 (Rehnquist, J., concurring).

26. *Id.* at 113 (Rehnquist, J., concurring).

27. *Id.* at 124 (Stevens, J. dissenting).

28. *See* Owen Fiss, *The Fallibility of Reason, in* Bush v. Gore: The Question of Legitimacy 84 (Bruce Ackerman ed., 2002).

29. 531 U.S. at 157 (Breyer, J., dissenting).

30. *Id.*

31. Moore v. Harper, 600 U.S. 1 (2023). In this case the Supreme Court addressed a decision of the North Carolina Supreme Court that set aside, as a violation of the state constitution, an enactment of the North Carolina legislature defining the boundaries of the Congressional district in the state. Accordingly, the provisions of the federal constitution in contention in that case was not Article II, but rather Article I, which allocates power to the states to determine the time, place, and manner of choosing members of Congress. Yet, the wording of Article II is similar to Article I, in that both refer to the state legislature to effectuate that allocation. The Court in *Moore v. Harper* refused to read that use of the word legislature to insulate state legislatures from review by state courts for compliance with state law.

CHAPTER 5

1. *See generally,* Alexander M. Bickel, *Minor Parties, in* Reform and Continuity: The Electoral College, the Convention, and the Party System 79 (1971).

2. *See* note 26 in Chapter 1. On these developments, *see generally,* Laura Kalman, The Long Reach of the Sixties: LBJ, Nixon, and the Making of the Contemporary Supreme Court 124 (2017).

3. 393 U.S. 23 (1968).

4. *Id.* at 35.

5. *Id.* at 30.

6. *Id.* at 32.

7. A similar regard for the impact on voters of state laws governing candidates is manifest in *Bullock v. Carter*, 405 U.S. 134 (1972). This ruling invalidated, under the Equal Protection Clause, a Texas law requiring candidates for local office in party primaries to pay high filing fees. The Court made a distinction, however, between state laws that limit the options available to voters and state laws that have a direct, exclusionary impact on voters, such as the poll tax invalidated by *Harper v. Virginia Board of Elections*. Accordingly, the author of the Court's opinion in *Bullock v. Carter*, the new Chief Justice Warren Burger, applied a test less exacting than the fundamental rights branch of strict scrutiny: "[T]he laws," he said, "must be 'closely scrutinized' and found reasonably necessary to the accomplishment of legitimate state objectives in order to pass constitutional muster." (Strict scrutiny, in its pristine form, requires the state's objective to be "compelling," not just "legitimate.") Burger saw filing fees as a means for eliminating spurious candidates and a means for financing primary elections, both legitimate objectives. He also insisted, however, that they were not the only means of achieving those objectives and thus failed the test of necessity. Burger wrote for a unanimous Court though, as in *Dunn v. Blumstein*, another 1972 decision, the two newest appointees, Lewis Powell and William Rehnquist, did not participate in the case.

8. 393 U.S. at 30.

9. *Id.*

10. 371 U.S. 415 (1963).

11. 393 U.S. at 30.

12. Notably, Black did not cite or in any way refer either to *Reynolds v. Sims* or *Harper v. Virginia Board of Elections*. Both are distinguishable from *Williams v. Rhodes*—*Reynolds* required equal population in the electoral districts used for the election of state officials; *Harper* struck down the payment of a poll tax as a condition for voting. Yet these decisions are no more distinguishable from *Williams v. Rhodes* than *Wesberry v. Sanders* and contain the same general language about the preciousness of the right to vote that appears in *Wesberry v. Sanders* and was quoted by Black in *Williams v. Rhodes*. In addition to *Wesberry*, Black cited *Carrington v. Rash*, a 1965 decision invalidating a Texas law denying military personnel stationed in the state the right to vote. See note 5 in Chapter 2. Justice Black dissented in *Harper* and his decision not to cite or refer to that ruling might have been

seen as a reaffirmation of his objection to it. His refusal to cite *Reynolds v. Sims* is more puzzling.

13. 393 U.S. at 38.

14. *Id.* at 39.

15. Although the peculiar origins of Douglas's opinion are suggested by the text of the opinion itself, for my account I greatly rely on the archival research of Jon A. Gryskiewicz. *See* Jon A. Gryskiewicz, *Williams v. Rhodes: How One Candidate, One State, One Week, and One Justice Shaped Ballot Access Law*, 28 J.L. & POL. 185 (2013).

16. 460 U.S. 780 (1983).

17. *Id.* at 786 n.7.

18. *Id.* at 789.

19. *Id.*

20. 393 U.S. at 39–40.

21. 460 U.S. at 794.

22. For the full quotation, *see* text at note 14 in Chapter 5 *supra*.

23. *See* OWEN FISS, LIBERALISM DIVIDED: FREEDOM OF SPEECH AND THE MANY USES OF STATE POWER (1996); OWEN FISS, THE IRONY OF FREE SPEECH (1998).

24. 504 U.S. 428 (1992).

25. In 1974, Justice White wrote the opinion of the majority in *Storer v. Brown* upholding a California election law that required independent candidates to be unaffiliated with a political party for at least a year before the primary of that party in the election year. The law was upheld on the theory that it contributed to political stability and prevented parties from fielding a short-term candidate to bleed off votes from a major political candidate. Justice Brennan wrote a dissent, joined by Marshall and Douglas, complaining that White had failed to apply the strict scrutiny test required by *Williams v. Rhodes*, because he did not consider whether those objectives could be attained through the use of less burdensome alternatives.

26. 504 U.S. at 445 (Kennedy, J., dissenting).

27. *Id.* at 438.

28. *Id.* at 445 (Kennedy, J., dissenting).

29. *Id.*

30. *Id.* at 444 (Kennedy, J., dissenting).

31. 460 U.S. at 789.

32. *Id.* at 806 (Quoting Kusper v. Pontikes, 414 U. S. 51, 58-59 (1973), Stevens ended, on this note, his justification for rejecting Ohio's early filing requirement: 'For even when pursuing a legitimate interest, a State may not choose means that unnecessarily restrict constitutionally protected liberty.' Dunn v. Blumstein, 405 U. S., at 343. 'Precision of regulation must be the touchstone in an area so closely touching our most precious freedoms.' NAACP v. Button, 371 U. S. [415], 438 [(1963)]. If the State has open to it a less drastic way of satisfying its legitimate interests, it may not choose a legislative scheme that broadly stifles the exercise of fundamental personal liberties."

33. 504 U.S. at 441 n.11.
34. 393 U.S. at 37.
35. 460 U.S. at 799 n.26.
36. 415 U.S. 709 (1974).
37. *Id.* at 719 n.5.

CONCLUSION

1. With a long sweep of history, reaching back to such foundational decisions as McCulloch v. Maryland (1819), Akhil Amar has persuasively argued for a "holistic reading" of the Constitution. AKHIL AMAR, AMERICA'S UNWRITTEN CONSTITUTION (2012).

2. It too is the subject of a pioneering case book, PETER M. SHANE and HAROLD H. BRUFF, SEPARATION OF POWERS LAW (1996).

Table of Principal Cases

. . .

General Index

...

For the benefit of digital users, indexed terms that span two pages (e.g., 52–53) may, on occasion, appear on only one of those pages.